THE

THE
INSIDE
STORY

ERIC MASON

PAN BOOKS
LONDON, SYDNEY AND AUCKLAND

First published 1994 by Pan Books Limited

a division of Pan Macmillan Publishers Limited
Cavaye Place London SW10 9PG
and Basingstoke

Associated companies throughout the world

ISBN 0-330-32990-1

1 3 5 7 9 8 6 4 2

A CIP catalogue record for this book is available from
the British Library

Typeset by CentraCet Limited, Cambridge
Printed and bound in Great Britain by
Cox & Wyman Ltd, Reading, Berkshire

Contents

Contents

CHAPTER ONE

George's Café
and the Porn Peddler

By the time I arrived at the strongbox I was barely conscious. I had been dragged bodily to the punishment block, the blows raining down on me while the screws pulling me along happily smashed my head against the iron stanchions holding up the landing above. The last thing I remember was a screw jumping on me while the baton-wielders were beating my testicles. I was beyond fighting back – all I could do was try to protect my body from the worst of their attacks. Eventually I must have passed out.

I woke up in the strongbox, strapped into a body belt. It felt as though every bone in my body was broken. My mouth was full of blood, the same blood that covered my whole body. In the dim light I could make out that I had no clothes on. I must have lain like that for hours – I was freezing cold and the pain was almost unbearable. At that point I was beyond caring whether I lived or died.

The next morning, about sixteen hours later, the screws came in and dragged me to the strongbox next door while the cleaner came down to mop up the blood. I was still caked in it and could hardly move when they told me to stand for adjudication. I just spat the blood out of my mouth as the Governor arrived with the Chief and stood in the doorway looking down at me as I lay naked on the floor.

Then off they went leaving me lying there. Later that day they came in with a bucket of water and washed me down like an animal, then dragged me back into the first cell I'd been in while their creepy cleaner cleaned up the other one. I knew that I had broken bones in my hands, and I had a severe pain in the lower part of my body and back which took many months to subside.

After two days with nothing to eat they finally brought a mess of goulash on a papier mâché plate and a cup of prison tea. My hands were still cuffed in the body belt so I couldn't use them. Instead I was forced to eat from the plate off the floor like an animal. I realized that one of my teeth had broken off in my gum when I went to pick the cup up with my teeth to tilt it. Although feeling more than a little depressed I was more determined than ever that I was going to beat them.

For about two weeks I was not allowed any access to a toilet and, not being able to use my hands, had to perform my bodily functions where I was. The screws dragged me from cell to cell, their cleaner following to clear up after me.

Eventually, eight screws came into the strongbox with a pair of slippers, trousers and a jacket about two sizes too big for me. They pulled the trousers on me and tied them round with a piece of mailbag rope, then wrapped the jacket right around me, buttoned it up and said, 'Visiting magistrates.'

Everyone was locked in their own cells while I was taken

to the boardroom. They didn't seem to mind the magistrates seeing me but they didn't want the other cons to witness my condition. The trial was farcical like they always were – typical kangaroo courts. After about five minutes I was taken back into the boardroom and told by the Chairman: 'Your punishment has been sent for recommendation to the Home Office.'

At midday about two weeks later, after everyone had been fed except me, the door of my cell was thrown open and about twelve screws stood outside. 'Take this prisoner to the laundry,' the Chief said. When I got to the laundry there stood the Governor and the doctor with their henchmen. The Governor wasted no time.

'The Home Office has confirmed your punishment. You will receive twelve strokes of the cat-o'-nine-tails and loss of six months' remission. Remove the prisoner's upper clothing and proceed to the frame.'

I was taken to the back section of the laundry. There stood a large wooden frame in the shape of a triangle. Next to this frame was an ordinary wooden table. On the table I saw firstly a large square of lint smeared with ointment, then a large canvas belt which I discovered was to protect my kidneys, a collar of soft material to protect my neck, and a long rectangular box which presumably held the cat-o'-nine-tails.

I had just taken all this in when my ankles were shackled to the legs of the frame and my wrists cuffed to two pulleys. My head was pushed through a slit in the canvas sheet attached to the frame and a cover was buckled over my head to stop me looking around to see who was flogging me. There was another canvas sheet attached to the left side of the frame to stop me seeing to that side. The pulleys were then pulled by two screws who took pains to avoid looking at me – perhaps they were squeamish. I could look to my right side where my 'friend' the doctor stood so that he could see both my face and back.

I heard the footsteps of the screw who was to administer the punishment. He came to the table. I could hear him open the box and take the whip out of it and I could hear the swish of the strands as he sorted them out. It seemed as though everyone was holding their breath, it was so quiet. I started to think about what Gibbsy had said to me, when he knew I was going to have the 'pussy': 'The first one hurts so much that it numbs your back and after that you can hardly feel anything.' It was some comfort.

So there I was in this atmosphere of silence and hatred, helpless and despairing because of my own frustration. I knew I had to take my punishment without a murmur to help me through my own private war against the system, a struggle that had started when, at the age of thirteen, I was sent to an approved school. I was now twenty-four years old, and a 'hardened criminal'. Sometimes I wondered how I had come to this.

I was born in St Mary's Hospital, Paddington, on 27 July 1930, the second of five brothers. Dennis was two years older than me, Fred and Brian two and five years younger respectively. Our youngest brother, Raymond, was not born until 1951.

My mother Margaret was a gentle person and I believe I was a bit of a favourite with her, although she loved all her boys and was proud of us all. For years she was convinced that I only got into trouble through taking the blame for other people – a belief that started during the War. My brother Fred, up to mischief again, had started a small fire in an air raid shelter. When the police came to investigate they were told that one of the Masons had done it. I said it was me rather than see my kid brother get into trouble – though everyone knew Fred was the culprit.

Unlike my mother, my father was a strict disciplinarian. My earliest memories of him are of being beaten with his thick leather belt. He was an ambitious man, proud of the fact that he was the chauffeur to the then Prime Minister, Ramsay MacDonald. He was also a good amateur boxer and it was through his interest in boxing that he met my mother, whose father and uncle were professional fighters – Jack, and Nick Foy 'The Marylebone Cyclone'. My father taught us to look after ourselves and to always fight fair. He would put boxing gloves on us and, kneeling on the floor, would make us try to hit him. Having to accept his counter-punches in return left quite an impression on us children.

But one event left an even greater impression on me. I can remember being in the house and hearing my mum screaming. Terrified, I ran downstairs, to see my father hitting her. I don't think I have ever got over witnessing that sight. My life has been violent at times but I have never hit any of the women I've had relationships with.

It was when I was about seven years old that I first became aware of how important boxing was in my family. My brother Dennis and I were allowed to get up at 3 a.m. to listen to the heavyweight Tommy Farr fighting Joe Louis on the radio. I remember how excited my father was when he thought Farr had won, only to hear the commentator declare Louis the winner and still champion of the world.

The arguments about who should have won seemed to be the only topic of conversation when anyone came to the house. (I was later to meet both of those great gladiators and tell them of my early memories.) About a year later I was to listen to another fight, which was reputed to be the greatest lightweight battle of all times, between Eric Boon and Arthur Danahar. Many years afterwards I met Eric Boon, who incidentally had something of a colourful life outside the ring. So it was no wonder that when my brothers and I used to put the boxing gloves on to spar with each other the sessions seemed to turn into a war of attrition, with both of us adopting the names of our current personal heroes.

It was later during the War, when my older brother Dennis, a pretty determined type, joined the Sea Cadets and began to box for them, that I became interested enough to do anything other than roam the streets and get into mischief. So I joined the Sea Cadets with my brother and we both boxed in the annual championships at Edgware Drill Hall, where our prizes were given to us by Admiral Sir Roger Keyes. We were so proud when we showed Mother what we had won – a gold-plated bosun's pipe. I think she'd have been happier if it had been a joint of meat, but our mother, like many other mothers during the War years, had to put on a bold front and somehow succeed in bringing up a large family up on a pittance.

I look back on those days with a certain nostalgia, although they were probably hard times for my mother. I remember how she used to get me to go to the grocer's to ask for three pennyworth of bacon bones so that we could always have a pot of bacon-bone soup simmering on the stove during the cold winters. She would send me because the grocer used to come to the amateur shows and sponsored some of the bouts, so he would always give me extra bones.

When the War started my father joined the Royal Army Service Corps as a driver and was quickly made a staff sergeant. With him no longer living at home, and rarely being able to visit us, life seemed a lot freer. Before the War we had moved from Marylebone into a council house a little way from where we had first grown up. I missed my grandparents and my cousins, who all lived near each other. My grandfather used to teach me to punch correctly, to cover up, move and build up my stamina, which was to stand me in good stead in later years. I was forever disappearing back to my grandparents and my mother got used to me not being around for days on end. I also loved to roam around on my own. I used to go on the Tube, buy a three-halfpence return ticket to the next station, then travel all over the Tube network for hours before returning home.

By 1941 the War was at its height, with bombing most nights and fighter planes having dog-fights in the clear skies over London during the day. By the time the air raid sirens sounded their warning after dark, most people would already be in the shelters or be getting ready to go down for the night. But I was usually to be found wandering around looking for good pieces of shrapnel to swap at school the next day, or on my way to my grandmother's

7

where I sometimes arrived around midnight before going to the shelter that had been dug between the blocks of flats. If it was the weekend there was invariably a party going on, plenty of beer for the adults and lemonade for the kids and plenty of cockney songs.

One night, on my way to my grandmother's, there was an air raid and I heard a bomb go off about a mile in front of me. I actually felt the blast and when I got to where the bomb had dropped, in the middle of the main road, the emergency services were helping people from the flats over the shops, which had all been damaged. One special constable asked if I was from one of the flats. 'No, I was bombed out further up the road and I'm going to my gran's,' I said. So he helped me by-pass the bomb crater and let me take a large tin of biscuits from a grocer's that had had its front blown in. By the time I got to the shelter in Marylebone I was a welcome guest with my tin.

I wasn't always allowed to get away with it, however. Christmas 1941 saw me travelling on the Tube for most of the day. I hadn't been home for a couple of days and when I arrived at Kennington Station the guard came and told us all to change as it was the last train. As I stepped on to the platform everyone by this time had claimed their pitch for the night and had already laid out their bed rolls. As it was Christmas, there were plenty of party hats, lemonade, mouth organs, accordions and singing. I thought, This will do for me, so I just stood there looking sorry for myself until somebody asked me, 'What's up, son?'

'I've been bombed out and I'm on my way to my gran's but the trains have stopped,' I replied.

Everyone rallied around: 'Poor little sod, give him something to eat and drink.'

I'd been enjoying myself, bursting with lemonade and cakes, when the old special came around.

'Poor sod, he's been bombed out, all his family killed,' they told him.

'What's your name, son?' he asked paternally.

'Eric Mason,' I replied.

'Are you from Edgware Road?' he asked suspiciously.

'Yes,' I said, before it occurred to me to wonder how he could know that.

It wasn't long before I was enlightened with a crack around the ear, and both myself and all the people who had been kind and sympathetic to me were to learn that half the police in London had been looking for me for once again worrying the life out of my mother by going missing. I was taken to the local nick, given plenty of verbal abuse and a few clouts around the head before being taken home. After an inquest at home it was decided that I would go to live in Marylebone with my grandparents.

It was OK at my gran's, but the school was no good for me. I was always fighting as I was deemed an outsider and there was only one way that kids settled their differences in that school. Eventually I was slung out of the school and had to go back to my mum's.

Luckily I found new friends: Arthur Holland, Eddie Sullivan, John Cooney and the Milsons. The Sullivan and Cooney families lived next door to each other, directly across the street from us. They always seemed to be feuding and it was the normal thing for everyone to come out on to the street whenever a row broke out between the two families. We were lucky to have a ringside view as our house was nearest to the flats where these two Irish families lived. One would frequently hear the cry 'The Sullivans and Cooneys are at it' and in no time the street would be full of spectators each supporting their particular family. I had no decision to make as my two best mates were Eddie and John. Those two got on very well and as a trio we went everywhere and did everything together.

By this time I was always breaking into and stealing from shops – mostly sweets and chocolates. It sounds bad but lots of kids from our background did the same. Then one day Arthur Holland told me that his mum's lodger, Tom, had hundreds of pounds in the house.

'Perhaps we should take some? He won't miss it if we only take a few,' Arthur suggested.

So it was arranged that I would go around to Arthur's house when Tom took Hilda out for a drink to the Stag. When the time came I went straight to Tom's room with Arthur, and there it was in a drawer – more money than I'd seen in my life. I took a handful – which it turned out to be £124; considering the average wage of a man was under £2 per week in those days, you can imagine how enormous the amount seemed when we got it to our den and counted it.

'Just give me one pound and you keep the rest,' Arthur said.

There was an old kettle in my dad's shed at home so I put £100 in that and the remaining £23 into my pocket. I couldn't wait for the morning to come to dash off to school.

I gathered all of the gang around me in the playground,

gave them all a ten-bob note apiece and said we'd all meet in George's café at dinner time. It was tea and pies all round.

'Who's paying?' demanded George when we placed our order.

'Don't worry, George, I'm paying,' I said grandly.

The bill for twelve teas and pies was about four shillings and eight pence, so I put a nicker on the counter and said, 'Keep the change.'

George was quick to catch on. He soon came around the counter. 'Do you want to buy this?' he said, lowering his voice.

'This' was a small metal box which, when one opened the front, revealed a figure of Jane, from the cartoon strip, with her little dog. As you turned the cog at the side of the box a man came towards Jane with no clothes on. George was the first porn peddler I was to meet. I gave him a nicker for it and took it back to school.

With the next day came a more realistic sexual encounter. We were all playing on and around the air raid shelters at school when a girl called Mary, who was sixteen, and who knew my older brother, came along. 'Tell Denny I'll see him at the arcade tonight,' she said.

I called her over and said, 'Look what I've got.' I showed her my little mechanical gadget and about £15 which I had in my pocket.

'Where did you get all that?' she asked, pointing at the cash.

'I've got hundreds,' I said, with plenty of bravado, as all my mates were there.

'Give me some,' she said.

'I'll give you some if you come down the shelter with me.'

'No, don't be so rude. I'll tell your brother what you said.'

'I don't care,' I shrugged.

But as she walked away she called me over and said quietly, 'I'll meet you after school but don't tell any of your friends.'

I made solemn promises, then went and promptly told all my mates as soon as she had gone.

After school had finished she came by with a loaf of bread under her arm as if she had just been shopping. I'd told my friends to pretend they knew nothing, but asked them all to come as soon as we went into the shelter.

'Don't leave me on my own with her,' I had begged them all.

'Grab the loaf and run down the shelter because I think all your friends know something,' she said.

Which I did. She came trotting after me into the shelter but then my bottle went and I didn't know what to do. My pals, who couldn't contain themselves any longer, came dashing in after us, which certainly saved my face. It was then that the suggestions started to come from out of the darkness.

'Lift her jumper up.'

'Lay her down.'

'No, you'll have to pay a shilling for a kiss and half a crown to touch anywhere,' she said swiftly.

Then she did her great actress bit by informing us that she was fainting and didn't know what was going on and couldn't feel anything happening to her. But she still had the presence of mind to keep taking money from me, as the boys commented on what was revealed.

'Look at the size of her tits,' an awed voice said from behind me.

I was certainly growing up quickly. Some days after this, and following other similar incidents, the police came to the school and interviewed about twenty kids. Eventually I was charged with stealing the money and about seventeen others for receiving part of it. In the course of being interviewed one of our neighbours enlightened the police about where most of the money was spent or given away, namely on the girl called Mary and at George's café. Both ended up in court; I believe George was sent to prison for a few months and the girl was sent away somewhere. I was fined ten shillings and my friends were each fined five shillings. I didn't worry too much as no one knew about the rest of the money left in the drum, but it certainly helped us through some pretty bleak days of food rationing and such.

By late 1943 Hitler had decided to bomb London out of existence and we had to endure a continual bombardment of his V1s and later V2 rockets. The V1s, which became known as 'doodlebugs', seemed to fascinate more than frighten us. As they were droning overhead we used to look at them and hope they would drop on the local sweetshop or somewhere else that would supplement our meagre rations. One day our dream came true when one landed on Kays toy factory off Edgware Road. I think just about every kid living within a mile radius descended on the factory. I remember my brother Fred and I were among the first to arrive, only to find a special constable minding the building. However, we soon realized he was, like most of the specials, a pre-War ex-policeman recruited to replace the ones who had been called up into the forces, who were not as nimble as we were. We spent nearly all day nipping in and out of Kays, dodging the bumbling attempts of the special to lay his hands on us and, in the mean time, getting plenty of games and other things to sell at school.

One of the most lucrative operations we had during the War came about as a result of the decision to get rid of the trams and take up the tram lines to use in the munitions factories. Once the workmen arrived they ripped up the tar blocks – blocks of wood set into tar to stabilize the tram lines – and piled the blocks at the side of the road before taking the tram lines away. The next day a lorry would come for the tar blocks but not before we got our hands on them. Every kid in Britain used to have a home-made trolley consisting of a plank of wood with two wooden axles and ballbearing wheels with an orange box screwed on the back and guide rope attached to the front axle. So we would make a few trips to the pile of tar blocks during the evening and take them back to the house, where we would spend hours chopping them into sticks, then into neat bundles. We would spend most of the weekend going around the houses to sell our firewood for a couple of coppers per bundle.

Less than a year later I was arrested again for breaking into a Home Guard ammunition store and stealing four boxes of hand grenades, detonators and bullets. One of the Milson brothers and I had decided to 'wag' school one day.

We took our trolleys with us, intending to load them with any ill-gotten gains we could find. We found a Home Guard store which was secured with an inadequate padlock and it wasn't long before we had the door open to discover, to our surprise, that the place was packed with dozens of boxes of ammunition. We had seen enough newsreel films to know how to arm the hand grenades so we packed as many as we could, together with their detonators, on to our trolleys and made our way back home. As my friend wouldn't risk taking any to his house in case his father found them, I deposited the load in my dad's shed. Later, when the coast was clear, I took a couple of grenades and a tin of detonators to my bedroom. I began the simple task of arming the grenades. This involved unscrewing the base of the grenades, inserting a detonator into the small holes inside and then screwing the base back on again. I couldn't wait for the next day to arrive so that I could show my friends what I'd got.

Next day, after debating what we should do with the grenades, it was decided that we would blow up the headmaster's office. As the evening began to close in we made our way to the park at the rear of the school. Right outside the head's office was a line of air raid shelters. We crouched behind them and myself and one of my friends each took a grenade. We drew the pins simultaneously, threw in approved military style towards the school, and quickly ducked back. The explosion brought us all back to our senses immediately. Luckily both grenades had missed the target and had fallen against the school wall. We did not have time to check what damage had been done as the explosion had alerted the ARP – Air Raid Precautions – warden. He immediately began to give chase but we were able to out-strip him easily and make our escape.

However, it was only a matter of time before the police arrived at my house. They frightened the life out of my mother when they told her that there were enough explosives in the shed to blow up the whole street. They also told her that it would only have taken the heat of one's hand to set off the detonators. I don't know whether that statement was true but it certainly had the desired effect upon my mother and she didn't argue when they took me away to the police station. For this crime I was sent to St Vincent's Approved School.

CHAPTER TWO

The German Prisoners were our Only Friends

Although it is easy to be wise in retrospect I think that St Vincent's decided the course my life was to take. The bullying, the physical and mental cruelty I suffered there at the hands of those in charge gave me a hatred of authority and a determination not to be beaten by their tactics that were to last all my life.

I was thirteen when I was sent to St Vincent's, an approved school run by monks which took in boys from the ages of ten to eighteen. The school had been evacuated in the early years of the War and was now located in a camp belonging to the Forestry Commission which looked like an Army barracks. My heart sank when I saw it and the reception committee did nothing to reassure me. The first thing they did was to give me a number, to be used instead of my name. My clothes were also stamped with this number and my peg in the shower room, on which I was to hang my clothes, was marked with it. In fact, each person was better remembered by their number than by their name, so those whose name I recall had some special reason to stand out. Mostly it was because they became good friends or they were characters who stuck in my memory for acts of bravado or bullies who I will never forget. There were a few who went through such misery without saying a word. It just amazed me how they could keep on taking it.

My introduction to the brutality came the first week I was there. Shortly after I arrived I was allocated to one of the eight dormitories, which slept sixteen. There was a rule which said that after eight in the evening there was to be no talking in the dormitories and I was caught whispering to the boy in the next bed by the dormitory leader, who was the oldest and biggest boy in the dorm. He could talk to his cronies as long as he liked but us new boys were ruled with an iron fist. I was told to stop talking and when I said, 'You're talking yourself,' it was as if I'd brought all the wrath of the gods down upon myself. No one would dare answer back to a dormitory leader. The next thing I knew I was being dragged from under the covers and ordered to stand at the end of the bed in my nightshirt until the brother came around to put the gas lamp out. I was freezing cold and I thought in my innocence that when he came in he would see I was shivering and feel sorry for me. What a rude awakening I was to get.

'What are you standing out for?' he bellowed.

'You'd better ask him,' I said, pointing to the leader, 'he's made me stand here in the cold just because I spoke a few words.'

With this, the brother punched me full in the face and split my eye. I dropped to the floor with the force of the blow. I'd never been hit so hard in my life. I was then ordered to stand up. I did. I couldn't believe what had just happened. I thought, he will now realize what he's done and feel sorry for me. I had a lot to learn. He just flattened

me again and said, 'If I find you standing out again when
I come around you will be birched.'

I was soon to learn there was no mercy in that place. I
had never had to worry about physical violence before. I
could look after myself. Boxing gloves were very familiar to
me as I had used them from an early age and, even when
we were kids, if we had a dispute we settled it with our
fists; if you got beaten there were no lasting grudges. But
St Vincent's changed all that for me. Firstly, when you
normally fight as a boy at school it is generally with a boy
of your own age and size, but not at St Vincent's. The
older, bigger boys were encouraged by the staff to discipline
the younger, smaller inmates. This gave the bullies a licence
to engage in the most brutal violence and perversions.
Obviously there were only three options for the victims of
these attacks: to fight back against impossible odds, to
suffer without a murmur, or to run away and then, when
you were brought back, get twice as much violence from
the staff. I can only talk with conviction about how I felt,
and how I decided I would face the next few years in St
Vincent's after I had tasted the first acts of brutality. I
knew I had to hold my head up high and never let them
see the slightest sign that I was going to give in.

The most traumatic experience in my early days at St
Vincent's was coming to terms with the sexual abuse. Like
most small boys I had discovered the delights of mastur-
bation and the pleasure of discovering what boys and girls
did with each other before I was sent away. But I had
never heard the word homosexuality and I had never met
anyone who was a homosexual. I was soon to learn how
rife it was in such institutions as St Vincent's. I've seen

sexual abuse by people who were in a position of authority and took advantage of that position either to bribe their way to gratify their own lust or, in quite a lot of cases, to force young boys who were too terrified to do anything about it. But I think the worse type of bullying and abuse came from the older boys against the younger, weaker ones. Whilst I was in St Vincent's, every night, after lights out, I would hear the sounds of the bigger boys forcing themselves on to the younger ones, the cries of resistance and then the prolonged sobbing of the victim. I spent the first year of my existence in St Vincent's lying awake until I just dropped off with sheer exhaustion and I think I had made it quite clear to any would-be molester that I was going to fight until I dropped rather than be bullied or abused. I obviously had the odd approach in the ordinary way but I was never tempted. The worst type of abuse came about when boys discovered that some poor little sod was a practising homo and was in fact enjoying himself. They would form a gang and subject that person to all kinds of abuses and perversions.

I had a very miserable few years there, but through all of the misery and pain there were the odd light moments and memories of the good mates that I had the good fortune to meet, some of whom I still see today. One of my best pals was Joey Mayo, a great character who sadly died of cancer many years ago. Joe and I had some terrible hidings in that place when we were young boys. Joe would do anything for a smoke and, as smoking was not allowed, it was the cause of quite a lot of grief for Joe – and for myself as, being his mate, I found myself involved on many occasions. One such incident was to get us one of the most severe beatings we ever had.

The lights had been out for about two hours when Joe came to my bedside and whispered, 'Meet me outside by the toilet.' I went out and found Joe standing there with a bootlace in his hand.

'Eric, I'm dying for a smoke,' he said desperately. 'I've managed to get some dog-ends from the staff room.'

He had risked a beating by going into the staff quarters to collect a few dog-ends from the ashtrays. Unfortunately he didn't have a light. So would I come with him to the church, where the sanctuary lamp was always burning, as he needed to climb on my shoulders to reach the lamp to light the bootlace. Once lit it would then smoulder for hours. I agreed and off we crept to the church, hoping that no terrible curse would come down upon us. Everything was going according to plan and Joe was kneeling on my shoulders, just putting the lace into the lamp, when I felt the most violent kick up my backside. I staggered forward while Joe went flying off my shoulders and landed on the altar. We were dragged out of the church and given a terrible beating. Unfortunately we hadn't realized that it was the practice of a few of the brothers to go to the church at night and sit in the darkness to pray and a couple of them had found us. But worse was to come.

The next morning everyone in the school was assembled in the recreation room to watch Joe and I be punished for sacrilege. We were both given a pair of skin-tight cotton shorts and told to take all our clothes off and put the shorts on. We were then put on the stage at one end of the recreation room and beaten on our backsides until blood ran down our legs. Those beatings were so severe that it took months for the wounds to heal. I had as many public beatings as anyone in the years that I was there. Some even overlapped and I hadn't even recovered from one beating before I was given another. There was a flagpost outside the Head's office and on more than one occasion Joe and I were tied to it and given a beating and subsequently left for several hours for everyone to see us as an example. I've been back recently and photographed what remains of that place and, although it's razed and obliterated, the post still stands as if it's a symbol of all that was evil about that establishment.

Poor gypsy Bennet, I think he suffered more than anyone. The poor guy wanted nothing more than to go into the woods surrounding the school and befriend the animal life that was there in abundance, everything from deer to wood pigeons. He was always arriving back with a young rabbit or a bird that couldn't fly. Unfortunately for him, he was always late for the count before meals and regardless of the weather, the rest of us would have to stand to attention until such time as he returned. As we were standing waiting the brothers would be inciting the boys with words like, 'Bennet needs a good hiding for keeping everyone from their meals,' and 'There will be no privileges this week, unless he's taught a lesson.' So by the time the poor sod came out of the woods, usually clutching some unfortunate bird with a broken wing, the whole school would be baying for his blood and the brothers just stood around as he was beaten up.

The only real kindness that I ever found while I was at

St Vincent's came from a strange quarter. At about the time the War was coming to the end we were all assembled and told that the prisoners from a German prisoner of war camp were coming on a kind of courtesy visit. None of us knew what to expect, as we had grown up with stories about what terrible people the Germans were. My father at that time was with the British Army of the Rhine and I had visions of him fighting hand-to-hand against these people we were supposed to make welcome and entertain with a display of sport, gymnastics, boxing and football. This was the face we were supposed to portray to our visitors – one big happy family that had been taken from the back streets of the big cities and made into gentle sports-loving people. But, whatever we expected it wasn't the sight of these smart-looking men, all with smiling faces and every one of them with a present to be given to us. In no time at all it was as if we'd recognized that we were kindred spirits, all of us missing our home life. Treasured family photographs were eagerly exchanged, and the language barrier did not exist in such a situation; family life was just the same whatever the country. The photographs were mainly of wives and chidren. Most of the Germans had children of our ages. Nostalgic times for everyone! The German prisoners started to come every weekend and we eagerly looked forward to their visits. They used to get a football team to play against us and some of them had played for top teams in Germany before the war. Some were musicians who would bring violins and such and play beautiful music.

Of course you could not hide all the physical signs of what people like Joe and myself were going through. I remember the German prisoners started to get concerned about our treatment after Joe and I had been whipped for one of our escapades. The usual thing, Joe had been down to the boiler house to light his bootlace and noticed that one of the kitchen windows was open. We always seemed to be starving hungry and the thought of finding some extra food was more than we could resist. We couldn't believe our eyes when we got into the kitchen for there was a big currant duff and two big tureens of custard. This must have been a Saturday night as we only had a sweet on Sundays. Well, Joe and I did no more than pull big chunks off the duff and while I was filling my shirt with big lumps of the stuff Joe had his head stuck right into the bowl of custard. We got back to the dormitory and woke up a couple of mates and gave them each a lump of duff then went to sleep. The next morning we were all tipped out of our beds and told to stand by them without moving. The brothers came straight up to our bed-spaces. It was then that I saw all the crumbs on the floor – at the same time that they did. They looked in disbelief at Joe, who had a big yellow ring of dried custard around his face. There were no words spoken, only the usual assembly and public beating. Later that day the Germans came for a football match and the whole place seemed more gloomy than ever. A few of them were looking at Joe and me with compassion in their eyes but when they saw the heavy weals and blood on the backs of our legs their mood changed to anger. I don't know if they ever complained about our treatment but we were never to see them again. We never knew why their visits suddenly stopped, but they were obviously aware that we were being ill treated. Without their visits life seemed much duller.

During the week there were classes. Brother Charles, the only brother who seemed to show some compassion, ran a class for those who were illiterate. As I had a smattering of education I was put into Brother George's class. It was his habit to prowl the classroom with an ebony ruler in his hand ready to rap your knuckles at the smallest excuse. At least there was a certain incentive to be moved up to Brother Raymond's class, where all one had to contend with was his sarcasm and ridicule. Unfortunately, once you had shown that you had a fair smattering of the three Rs you were sent to the workshops, which were Dickensian. I seemed to spend all my days sandpapering planks of wood until my hands were sore. The instructor was a crack shot with wooden missiles that he would throw at anyone not working hard enough.

We had an hour of recreation time in the evening and in the summer we'd play football and other games on an adjoining field. We were free on the weekends, once we'd done our chores such as scrubbing the dormitory, cleaning the windows and tidying up outside. On Sundays, of course, we went to church – twice, once in the morning and again in the afternoon. I don't think much of this religion rubbed off on us though.

As the years went by I grew bigger and fitter. The War was nearing its end and I was spending nearly all of my time training and had been picked, along with a couple of other boys, to represent the school in the Home Office Boxing Championships. My personal suffering seemed to abate a little. I was beginning to rebel a bit and there were a lot of easier pickings for the bullies and staff. My rebellion was sparked off when the instructor in the wood shop hit me with one of the missiles he was so fond of throwing. I'd finally had enough and for the first time I hit back, hurling a sanding block at him. He came running towards me, throwing punches. I started to trade blows with him and although he was bigger and stronger than myself I could see that I had shocked him. I was severely flogged for this but he never threw anything at me again.

One boy I became very friendly with in those days was Joe King. He was a very good boxer though after he left St Vincent's it was as a singer that he made a living. His brother, Peter King, was to fight Peter Waterman, the brother of Dennis Waterman, for the British welterweight title. I went on to win my weight division in the Home Office Championships at Chelsea Barracks, where I was to meet a boy from another school with whom I became very friendly years later. His name was Jimmy Lynas, 'The Coventry Iron Man'. He was later to become the first man to beat Dick Tiger, who was to go on to become the middleweight champion of the world.

I seemed to get a new status after my return from Chelsea Barracks and I didn't have to join in the forced route marches the boys had to endure. I hated those marches as we were expected to walk about ten miles through country lanes in boots which were ill-fitting and sometimes without laces. There was absolutely no reason for these marches and I can only presume that it was enforced purely to gratify the sadism of the people who ran the home. At the end of the 'walks' as they called them, there would be the ritual of bursting blisters or bathing bleeding feet.

It was at this time that I had my first sexual experience.

It came about when, as one of the more senior boys, I was allowed to go to the local carnival with the gym team. It was at a village three miles from the school and we were to give a gymnastics exhibition for the locals. As soon as the exhibition ended we were allowed to mingle with the villagers and to my surprise I found myself being invited to walk into a field next to the one in which the carnival was being held. In no time at all I was indulging in the kind of things that I had only been able to dream about until then. When I got back to the school I was soon telling my pals about the beautiful girl that I'd met and the things that I'd done. As soon as I'd finished describing her they all said, 'Yeah, we know her, every older boy in the school has had the pleasure.' That certainly gave my ego a jolt as I thought I was her first lover.

CHAPTER THREE

Soho, the Snake Pit and All that Jazz

I was discharged from St Vincent's in 1946 and given a train warrant back to London, where I thought I'd get a job, settle down, join a good boxing club and live happily ever after. My dad was back from the Army, Dennis was in the Navy and Fred and Brian were at school. I expected to get a job and contribute towards my keep. I didn't ever fancy going through the type of life I'd had for the last three years again. So it was with great expectations that I went looking for my first job. But like all good plans, there always seemed to be a pitfall and the first difficulty came when I was asked, 'Where did you work before?'

As everyone from our walk of life left school at fourteen and went immediately into a job, the fact that I was sixteen and hadn't worked needed explaining. I had no option but to tell people that I'd been in an approved school for three years. After the interviewers had obtained all the details from me they'd either tell me straight out that there wasn't any work or they'd let me know in more subtle ways but the end result was the same.

With nothing better to do I took to sitting around in well known cafés in Soho – Queenie's, the Little Hut and the Snake Pit. Most of the girls that frequented these places were prostitutes and I always remember them with fondness. I'd invariably have a meal or a cup of tea sent over to me whenever any of them came in and in due course I felt protective towards them, although some were old enough to be my mother. There would be some sort of incident each day. Either a punter would arrive screaming that a girl had 'rolled' him, left him with no trousers on while she made off with his money, or one of their ponces would come in pissed and demand money for more booze. I would always 'make one' and rarely had any difficulty in knocking these individuals out so I became a great favourite with the girls around the West End.

At this time I was meeting all kinds of villains. Jack Spot was the 'name' both in the East End and the West End. Jack had made quite a name for himself by championing the Jews against Oswald Mosley's Blackshirts, and by this time was a pretty well-respected villain and well organized. I used to see Jack and several of his 'firm' in those days. Many had girlfriends who were 'brasses', so I got the odd bung (money) from a few faces.

Jack made a fortune from the many rackets that he ran; one of the most lucrative was the Bookmaker's Sponge. It was so very simple and yet so financially rewarding. It worked like this: as each bookmaker set up his pitch, for which he was licensed, he would erect his blackboard and list the various horses running in each race. As the prices fluctuated throughout the betting the bookie would rub out the old odds and replace them with the new. At the 'off' the boards would be wiped clean ready for the next race. Jack decided that he would supply the bookmakers with their sponges – at an exorbitant price of course. If any bookie refused to take one of Jack's sponges he would find himself trying to carry on conducting his business while a gang of hard men fought around his pitch. On many such occasions the bookie would be knocked down in the mock battle along with all of his equipment.

When it became known that Jack was making plenty of money from the tracks around London, the organized gangs from the North and the Midlands wanted to get in on the act. So Jack became the guardian angel of all of the southern bookies who went to the race tracks up and down the country. During the thirties and forties the race course fights between underworld gangs made the headlines, with the razor slashings and general violence getting out of hand. It all culminated in a famous battle at Brighton race track where the Sabini brothers, a well-known Italian family, became involved. There were a number of arrests and plenty of hard labour was dished out to all concerned, but Jack Spot came through it all to be acknowledged as the 'Governor'. He set himself up as London's very first gang leader. He had a lifestyle to match, with big cars, expensive suits and attractive women. He eventually set up his headquarters in a hotel at Marble Arch, where he could be seen every night holding court with his right-hand men, Moisha Blue Ball and Sonny the Yank, and there was always plenty of coming and going. The waiters who worked there in those days were getting more money in tips than the manager of the hotel earned in salary.

It all came to an end for Jack after his fight in Frith Steet, Soho, with Albert Dimes – Italian Albert. They ended up cutting lumps out of each other and were both arrested for an affray. But it became known as the fight that never was after a retired vicar arrived at the Old Bailey with an entirely different story from the one given by the prosecution and the case was dismissed. If any member of the jury had gone to the bar in Jack's hotel that evening they would have seen the vicar swallowing plenty of champagne and brandy with guys from Jack's firm. But from then on it was all downhill for Jack. He was accused of slashing a guy but he had been set up. The victim had his arm slashed by his own friends and then gave evidence that Jack had done it.

The last time I saw Jack it was in a club in Bayswater in about 1966. As I rang the door bell I could see someone looking through a slit in the door and could hear several bolts being pulled. It was like a fortress. Jack had been attacked just prior to this and had given evidence against the perpetrators, who were sentenced to long terms of imprisonment. It spelled the end of Jack Spot's reign as the underworld boss. He had forgotten the old maxim – 'If you live by the sword, you die by it.'

Soho in the late forties and early fifties was a unique part of London, full of fascinating characters. In the summer evenings people would sit outside the open doors of their premises and everyone seemed to know each other. The girls who worked the streets would click up and down on their stiletto heels, greeting everyone with a cheery hello and 'I've got to get a few quid tonight as the rent's due tomorrow.' You would see the buskers pull up in their cars and stroll down to Leicester Square to do the soft-shoe shuffle or mimic the sand dancers in the middle of the road. The one-man bands and street singers all added to the attractive atmosphere. One great character who used to stroll through Soho, if he wasn't at a race meeting, would be Prince Monolulu. He was an imposing black man who always wore flowing robes and a feathered head dress. As he walked he would chant his cry, 'I've gotta horse.'

One of the great characters, who I have known for over thirty years, was Charlie Dice. Charlie, who used to train in the East End, was a very fit and strong man. He made his living in the illegal 'speilers' (gaming clubs) or in the street dice games which were a feature of London right up to the sixties.

People would travel for miles to play dice in the street. I've seen men win fortunes in a couple of hours crouching down outside the Little Hut café in Greek Street, Soho. When Billy Gardner and Charlie ran the games in Soho the police tried in every way possible to catch them, but their look-out system was too good. The police couldn't get within a hundred yards before the warning was given and the gamblers either dispersed or were discovered sitting innocently in the Little Hut having a cup of tea.

But the police scored a victory one night. There was a big game on at the time and nobody took any notice of the council dust cart trundling down the street. If anyone had looked harder they would have noticed that there were twice as many dustmen as usual. But no, everyone was used to seeing the dust cart at 3 a.m. so the look-outs were relaxed as the vehicle pulled up alongside. The dustmen, who were all from Savile Row Police Station, pounced and grabbed the dice and what money they could and nicked most of the guys involved. Everyone appeared at Marlborough Street Magistrates' Court the next morning and were fined sums from £2 up to £5 for the organizers.

In fact, if you were feeling bored and in need of cheering up, all you had to do was go to any of the courts within a mile of Soho for some free amusement. There were three of them working flat out and you would see the same old faces day after day. The girls would turn up in all their furs and finery, say good morning to the magistrate, who would reply, 'Good morning, Sonia' – or whatever the girl's name was – and immediately give them the maximum fine for prostitution, which was £2.

Then there were the fly pitchers, the guys who sold gear out of a suitcase on the pavement in Oxford Street. This was much more serious than prostitution and would involve a £5 fine. There was a lot of good humour in the courts and after their appearance everyone would meet in Queenie's café, in Rupert Court, for breakfast before going home to bed to get ready for the evening's work.

The place that I enjoyed the most in those days was the Club 11. I was to see all the great jazz men of the day playing there: Ronnie Scott, Tubby Hayes, Lennie Bush. I could name dozens of great musicians who played the old Club 11 and I watched a lot of them become famous, seeing them years later in Ronnie Scott's place in Gerrard Street and Frith Street. I had some good times with Tony Crombie and Alan Haven when they used to tour with Wee Willie Harris and there was always some place to go after the show for a drink.

It was in the Club 11 that I first heard of drugs. The place was packed with happy jazz fans one evening when our numbers were suddenly swelled by hordes of policemen. I noticed everyone around me was throwing little paper packages on to the floor. We were all rounded up and taken down to the local nick and searched. It didn't matter whether you had anything on you or not, because the police had picked up all of the packets from the floor – which contained marijuana, called Indian Hemp – and if there was someone there who didn't have any they would soon see that they were suitably 'fitted up' with some. Those of us who were in our teens were given a ticking off and asked for our names and addresses, which we all quickly supplied, giving them fictitious ones, before being allowed to go. But sadly some of our heroes were sent to prison for three years.

I was also training quite regularly. Every day I would go to Kline's gym in Fitzroy Square but on the odd occasion I would go down to Jack Solomon's gym where I could pick up a few quid for sparring with the Americans who came to fight British boxers. Most of the great American fighters who came to this country would train at Solomon's in Windmill Street, except for Sugar Ray Robinson. When he came to the UK to fight Randolph Turpin he trained at Windsor. Most of these guys from the States had pretty large contingents of followers, managers, trainers and sparring partners who would always be on the bill. Robinson went overboard with his own hair dresser, manicurist and valet; he even had a 'midget'. He had over fourteen people in his entourage but it didn't help him, he still lost the middleweight title in that epic fight at Earl's Court. It was a great day for British boxing when they held Turpin's hand up after the fight. Freddie Mills had lost the light heavyweight title to Joey Maxim earlier the same year and so it made Turpin's win that extra bit special.

But I was still looking for the cloud with the silver lining. It didn't matter how many rounds I sparred or boxed I wasn't going to get the type of money that I needed. I was looking for more and chance showed me how to find it.

On my way home from Jack Solomon's gym I'd sometimes pop into the snooker hall on the first floor of the same building for a cup of tea or a soft drink. It was a popular haunt for smash-and-grab raiders who would meet their fences there. I'd watch these guys with their wads of money bet heavily on the games of snooker. The word soon got out and every hustler in London seemed to find his way to the Windmill snooker hall. A lot of these raiders knew that I used the gym upstairs. It suited them to have a fit person on the team – and I let it be known that I was willing to join them.

It wasn't long before I started to learn the ropes. It was simple. Smash-and-grab raids on jewellers' shops were the most popular way of making easy money in those days and without unbreakable glass all the jewellers' shops were at the mercy of the daring raider. 'Ringing' cars was as commonplace then as joyriding is today so there was always a car available with false plates.

All we would have to do was look for a display where the pads of rings were easily accessible then drive the car up to the shop, pointing the front right into the doorway with the engine running. Moving fast we'd take our 'lump hammer', make a hole at the bottom of the window, reach in with a long bar we called the 'cane' and 'cane the burnt' – burnt cinder being rhyming slang for window. The 'burnt' would come out with a crash on to the pavement below, leaving us to pull as many pads out as we could, stuffing them into a canvas bag we took with us. Everything we did was at top speed, adrenalin pumping, hurrying each other along, ears straining for the sound of police whistles. In less than a minute we'd be off, driving to the nearest Tube station if we hadn't been followed. We'd dump the car round the corner and get on the first train, regardless of where it was going. At that point we'd be high with excitement, relief making us laugh at anything.

The more windows you smashed the more expert you got at it. Eventually, you could take a window out without covering all the jewels with broken glass, or as I'd done on many occasions previously spending an hour or so afterwards taking slivers of glass from your head. We loved to read the papers after we'd had a particularly exhilarating chase with the police and managed to evade capture. The headlines used to read 'Wizard of the Wheel' and then go on to describe a dramatic chase across London after an especially daring raid on a jeweller's.

I was now starting to pal about with different West End faces. One was Chic Joyce who was later to get a life sentence for a fight where a guardsman died. Most of the guys wanted to go to the dance halls like the Lyceum or Hammersmith Palais, the Royal or the Paramount in Tottenham Court Road. It was in the Paramount that I made a bit of a name for myself. I was seventeen at the time and I felt that a guy was paying too much attention to my girlfriend. An argument broke out and I hooked him to the chin. He went down as if he had been pole-axed. I was to read later in the paper that the Empire featherweight champion had been knocked out in the Paramount dance hall.

It was a strange life for a teenager to live and I loved the danger and the excitement, the feeling that we were pitting our wits against the law and winning. I was also enjoying a new independence, having moved out of my parents' house to a flat in Frith Street. But every so often my brother Fred would search me out in the West End with the message that the 'old lady' was worried about me so I'd go home for a short visit. I tried to keep what I was doing from her – otherwise she really would have been worried!

It was about this time that I started to break into places like cigarette shops, milk depots and bakers' depots, usually with an accomplice. One of my best friends was a guy called Teddy Bright, a well-known 'tea-leaf' (thief) and a lovable rogue. He lived in the next street to my parents and we were forever getting up to some kinds of villainy. We used to sit in Ted's house and plan our future money-making schemes, with a little bit of encouragement from Ted's mother. They made a great team. Ted, who took everything in his stride, looked on crime as an ordinary occupation, as normal as working in a factory. And his mum had the same attitude. If he needed to get up early to do a break-in she would wake him up in time and have his gloves and jemmy all ready for him.

One particular day I was telling Ted something that I had overheard my father talking about. My father had gone into business, with a partner, in the fruit and veg trade. They had a pitch next to the local fish shop whose owner was running a football pontoon scheme. All of the local traders were putting money into it and it had now gone about seven weeks without there being a winner. My father reckoned that if he won it there would be a few hundred quid to collect.

Ted and I deduced that all this money would have to be

in the office of the fish shop and we decided it would have to be 'done' before someone won it. We decided to break in that very moment, a Sunday lunch time. We had no trouble getting into the place as there was an iron staircase leading to a veranda and once on the veranda it only took us a minute to get through the window into the office. To our disappointment we found a small safe. We searched the rest of the place but no money came to light so it had to be in the safe. Ted and I knew nothing about opening safes, in those days, but we thought if we could get it safely away we would be able to force it open. First we would need a car and we knew that the local Catholic priest had one in his little lock-up garage which he never used on a Sunday. We decided to borrow it.

We soon had the priest's car rolling towards the back of the fish shop, where we left it and went back inside the office. We had a bit of a job lifting the small safe through the window and on to the veranda but once there we quickly moved it across the veranda to the top of the iron stairs and pushed. It made a terrible racket as it bounced down and we hurriedly manhandled it into the boot of the car. We couldn't close the boot lid so we decided to get away from the shop in case someone came to see what all the noise was about. Ted was driving as we came out on to the Edgware Road and passed a queue outside the picture house. We knew practically everyone in that queue and we could see them all pointing at the back of the priest's car where the safe was sticking out. We lost no time in turning off into a side-street where we tied the boot down over the safe with the laces from my shoes.

We eventually arrived at a place which was a lovers'

lane at night but in the day time was nearly always deserted, and set about the back of the safe using the railings torn from the park fence and a tyre lever. But we couldn't open it and so decided to leave it hidden in the bushes and go for some more sensible tools. We obtained a jemmy, a lump hammer and a big chisel from the builder's yard at the back of Ted's house and went back to our task. It wasn't long before we had the back off the safe and after that the inner casing was easy. We were soon lifting the money. We were lucky, not only the football money but the shop takings from Friday evening and all day Saturday were inside. We took the money back to Ted's house, where his mother helped us count it. We gave her all of the silver and coppers and split the notes between ourselves, then returned the priest's car and got tidied up ready to get down the West End to see the bright lights.

The next day my father was fuming. He came in from work saying some villains had broken into the fish shop and nicked all of the football money. He described what he would do if only he could get his hands on them – which worried me more than the police finding out. I started to think of all of the people who had been queueing for the pictures and wondered uneasily how long it would be before they put two and two together and started gossiping. But strangely nothing ever came of it, although I know my father did suspect Teddy Bright as he said to my mum one evening, 'That young Brighty had something to do with that break-in at the fish shop. His mother's been in the Stag every evening this week and I know she always gets a share of his ill-gotten gains.'

Shortly after this Ted and I went our separate ways and

I wasn't to see him until I met him in Dartmoor where he was doing seven years for sticking up a bank. His accomplice was his girlfriend. The papers called them the modern Bonnie and Clyde.

CHAPTER FOUR

Bread and Water and the Strait-jacket

Perhaps because I was so young, I never worried about being caught. I was enjoying life and saw no reason why I shouldn't carry on stealing and living it up with the proceeds. I was to have a rude awakening when I was finally arrested for store breaking and stealing cigarettes, spirits and cash to the value of £3,000 and remanded to Wormwood Scrubs. That was my first look into a prison and it was a pretty horrendous experience. The first thing that struck me, like a physical blow to the stomach, was the terrible stench of urine and excreta that permeated the whole prison, lingering even in your clothes. I never got entirely used to it. The cons would empty their slop buckets out of their cell windows and the contents would linger in the yard until the screws detailed someone to clean it up. As for the toilets, it was necessary to take a deep breath before entering them otherwise the smell would make you vomit. The screws spoke to the prisoners as if they were the scum of the earth. You were not allowed to talk to anyone and if you answered the screws back you would soon find yourself on bread and water.

After being sentenced to three years' Borstal I was immediately taken back to Wormwood Scrubs Prison to await allocation to whatever Borstal I was to serve my time at. I had already had my card marked as to the reception I was going to get if I was sentenced because of my verbal run-ins with a few of the screws whilst on remand. They had to be a bit careful until I had been sentenced. It wouldn't do for me to go to court with the marks of a beating all over me, so they settled for verbal abuse and general harassment, putting me on report for the most trivial of offences – and there were hundreds of ways they could do that even though you were locked in your cell for twenty-three hours a day.

I was, therefore, expecting to have problems when I got back into Wormwood Scrubs but I was still surprised by the way it happened. Trouble came the first morning after being sentenced. When they brought the breakfast to the cells – a cup of watery tea, a cob of bread and a plate of porridge – we would also get a spoonful of sugar, which we normally kept to eke out between our breakfast and cocoa later on. This time the screw just pulled my door shut without giving me any sugar, so I yanked the bar that rang the bell. I could hear them shouting, 'Who's ringing that bell?' though they could see who it was, as the tally outside your door would drop down when you pulled the bell bar. They ignored me until everyone had been served then three or four of them came to my cell and said, 'What are you ringing that bell for?'

'I've not had any sugar,' I replied.

The screw who'd shut the door said, 'You put it in your tea.'

'You know that I was never given any,' I said.

With that he lashed out with his fist. That was the signal

for them all to jump on me. I was taken, still struggling, to the strongbox at the end of the wing and thrown inside. As the doors shut behind me I looked around. There were a few tiny panes of unbreakable glass set high up in the wall which allowed in a little light from the gas lamp set behind them. A grill, over the door allowed in some air. The only furniture was a bed made up of a board set in concrete. There were no blankets.

When the two reinforced doors leading into the strong-box were shut it was almost entirely sound-proof. Sometimes you would hear the reverberation of doors slamming elsewhere in the prison, but that was the only other sign of life.

I was left alone until dinner time, when the sharp grating of the key in the lock of the outer door announced the arrival of the screws. I braced myself, remembering the threats they had uttered before shutting me in – threats it would be all too easy for them to carry out in this isolated cell. It took six of them to bring me my dinner, which was contained in a can about 8 inches tall and about 5 inches in diameter. The contents appeared to be some watery soup with something that looked like rubber floating in it. This was the well-known 'floating duff' which was served in all prisons at that time.

I was also given a charge sheet that said I would be accused of gross personal violence against a prison officer. As I read it I knew that no one was ever found not guilty of any charge, so with nothing to lose I thought I might just as well let them see that I wasn't so easily beaten. Without warning I flattened one of the screws who had given me the trumped-up charge. Within a very short time I was feeling very sore and was securely strapped into a strait-jacket – for what was to be the first of many times.

I was eventually sentenced to fifteen days No. 1 diet and forty-two days No. 2 diet for my alleged attack on a prison officer and taken back to the strongbox. The No. 1 diet was served as three days on bread and water with one day off until you'd served your fifteen days. Then you'd start your No. 2 diet when your bread and water would be supplemented with porridge and two potatoes. This would be seven days on and three days off until you'd served your forty-two days. There would be no furniture in your cell, just three boards of wood set in concrete and they would give you a papier-mâché receptacle to put your drinking water in. During all this time I had not been allowed to wash, so when the Governor came around I asked him if I could have permission to clean myself. He ordered: 'Get this man washed up.'

A little later a screw came in with a couple of his friends and said, 'I've got a present for you; it's a bar of soap, compliments of the Governor.'

With that he dropped the bar of carbolic soap into my drinking water and left, saying, 'Get cleaned up.'

After about three or four months of complete misery in that place, I was told I'd been allocated to Portland Borstal. This I expected, as it had the reputation of being the hardest place in the British penal system. I was soon to find out that nothing had been exaggerated.

Portland Borstal was situated on a peninsula of the coast of Dorset and it had been in the past one of the most notorious prisons in the old days of penal servitude and hard labour. It was where Charlie Peace, one of the more infamous characters in Madame Tussaud's House of Horrors, did his time with a ball and chain around his ankle.

The punishment block had been used to house the old lags in years gone by. It still had an atmosphere of gloom and despair. I was to spend a few months in that block whilst I was in Portland. The ordinary time spent in Portland was bad enough, with the spartan regime and the hard work. But the punishment block was something else. If you were sentenced to a period in the Block, as it was known, your day went as follows. At 6 a.m. you would fold your bed neatly and on being unlocked you would take your bedding to a rack at the end of the Block. Then you would fill a bucket full with cold water and taking carbolic soap and a scrubbing brush scrub every inch of your cell. You would then clean the bucket and put it back where you got it from. Next you would line up and be marched out into the yard at the back of the Block, regardless of what the weather was like, where you would do half an hour of physical training. This would be repeated five times during the day, only interrupted by the job of sawing railway sleepers into logs for chopping into sticks for the screws' fires. By 4.30 p.m. you would be back in your cell to be given a couple of pairs of handcuffs that had been lying in water for a couple of days to make them rusty. It would be your job to polish them until they shone. When you had finished, and they were gleaming, they would be put back into the water to start the process over again. At eight o'clock you would be allowed to go and get your bedding and take it back to your cell.

The ordinary spartan regime was equally monotonous

except for the weekends which were very good if you liked sport, and I looked forward to them with great anticipation. We indulged in most sports but they limited boxing to the odd bout between two guys from different houses who had the reputation of being the best in the place. With these official fights everyone would go down to the gym to see the outcome but most of the differences were settled in a cell or in the toilets. I met some pretty tough people whilst I was there.

The worst part of being in Portland, the thing that I still think of with horror, was the Burma Road. That was our place of work and it was just as hard as the name implies. The idea behind the Burma Road was a good one. The aim was to turn the barren land near by into sports fields, and before I arrived the old quarry had been converted into the stadium. It was one of the best sports grounds that I had seen. However, I could vividly imagine the suffering that had occurred whilst the quarry had been transformed into the pride and joy of the Home Office. Visitors were invariably taken to see the stadium to show what the Borstal boys had created for themselves for their own recreation. But no one was ever told of the real feelings of the boys involved, who had to work with blistered and bleeding hands whilst the screw stood in close attendance to ensure that the rocks were removed and the earth thrown at the riddles. Absolute silence was the principal rule and the screws made sure that nobody talked.

There were many men who couldn't face another day on the Burma Road and they would inflict injuries on themselves. Some that couldn't do it to themselves would ask their mates to do it. It was nothing to walk into the wash house and see some poor individual having his arm broken. I remember a guy having a pickaxe put through his foot. He was crippled for life.

The team that I worked with there were a pretty hard bunch. There were four of us: Alfie Burns from Manchester, Ronnie Smith from Battersea, Tam McGrory from Glasgow and myself. Alfie was a very big guy with a mop of blond hair who was always in trouble with the authorities and the house captain for refusing to get his hair cut. He loved his sport and although he wasn't the fastest athlete in the world he was like a brick wall in defence at football. We would play a game called 'murder ball' which involved no rules whatsoever. Alfie Burns loved that game. Two teams consisting of anything from six to twelve players on each side would endeavour, at the whistle, to get a medicine ball over the opposing team's defensive line starting from a spot mid-way between the two dead ball lines. One could use any method to achieve this objective. A favourite ploy would be for one of the team to wrap himself around the ball whilst the rest of the team tried to drag him over the opponents' line. Meanwhile the other team would try to drag the guy the other way. Murder ball was a real test of physical endurance.

It wasn't long after Alfie Burns had been released from Portland that he was charged with murder, together with another Mancunian named Devlin. It became known as the 'Burns, Devlin case' and they were the last two people to be hanged at Walton Prison in Liverpool.

Ronnie Smith was a very tough guy indeed. I later met his brother Les whilst in Wandsworth Prison and by that time other members of the family were becoming well known. Tam, the other member of the quartet, had been sent to Portland following a riot in the top Borstal in Scotland. He arrived with a very big reputation but he turned out to be quiet. It soon became clear, however, that his quietness was not because he feared what Portland had to offer. His theory was that if you left people alone you would not be bothered by anyone yourself. Unfortunately for him things didn't work that way. There was always someone ready to test the water. The first guy who wanted to test Tam's strength was called The Bull. He was a big rough-looking man who would eat about a gallon of porridge every morning. He was absolutely despicable in every way, stank of BO and never washed. But the day he tried his hand with Tam was the biggest mistake of his life. Tam gave him a real beating and then dumped him in the shower – which I think hurt The Bull even more. This event was just one of the many small interruptions in our normal life which was dominated by the back-breaking tasks on the Burma Road.

It was after a particularly hard day at this work that Tommy Williams approached me with a plan to escape. It wasn't much of a plan but I think I would have taken any chance to break away from the hardship and monotony. Tommy had worked in the fitter's shop and whilst there had made a key which would start most cars. It looked like an old Lucas key, made from a flat piece of metal shaped like a spade. It was normal practice every weekend for the boys to be taken to the sports field, situated outside the rear wall of the institution, to participate in some inter-house sporting activity. We all looked forward eagerly to these events and the screws would 'psych' the boys to fever pitch to ensure that their own house won as many tournaments as possible. There were five houses named after great naval heroes and I guess any boy who passed through Portland just after the War will recall those confrontations between the various houses until his dying day.

Now to fall in with Tommy's plan I had to feign an injury in order to exclude me from taking an active part in the forthcoming weekend sporting events. Tommy had spotted a car which was parked outside the old quarry-master's house at the top of the sports field. The idea was that, given a fair bit of luck, we should be able to slip over the fence and make it to the car whilst everyone's attention was directed towards the inter-house tug-of-war contests. Tommy thought that if we were able to get a couple of minutes' start we could get to the car and drive down to Chesil Beach. If our luck held and we were off Portland Bill before the screws could phone the police, who would then close the roads, we should have a good chance of getting away. It was well known that the only possible escape was via the road over Chesil Beach. There had been numerous attempts by boys to swim away but many of these had ended in near-disaster due to the treacherous local currents.

As the time approached for us to make our break we walked slowly towards the quarry at the top of the sports field, whilst everyone else's attention was focused on the tug-of-war teams who were about to battle it out. As soon as we heard the referee shout, 'Take the strain. Heave,' Tommy and I went over the fence and ran towards the parked car.

To our dismay we heard the screws shout, 'Two away,' and we were chased immediately. But we got to the car before the screws crossed the quarry and the engine fired into life at the first pull on the starter.

We were away. It now became a matter of urgency to get across Chesil Beach before the police were notified and closed the road. As we drove down the steep hill towards Weymouth we saw one of the off-duty screws trudging up the hill. With freedom so close we gave him a cheery wave. He was just about to respond when he realized that it was two escapees. He nearly had a fit, shaking his fist and stamping his feet.

Tommy and I were in a very buoyant mood when we got to Chesil Beach and found that there were no road blocks. We went flying through Weymouth and nearly mowed down a group of people waiting at a bus stop. Then we made a very fundamental mistake. We tried to drive straight through to Dorchester instead of abandoning the car where it would not be found for some time and then lying low until darkness. Not long out of Weymouth we heard the familiar ringing bell of the old Wolseley police car. Turning round, I reported that we had a couple on our tail.

We both waved in a fit of bravado.

'Right,' I said briskly to Tommy, 'let's lose them.'

He speeded up but we couldn't shake them off. We soon decided we would have more chance on foot so we abandoned the car and struck off across the fields. The chase began and we were clearly out-distancing the pursuers. We were just starting to feel hopeful again when, looking up, we saw another posse up ahead cutting off our escape. We were soon captured and returned to the Borstal. As soon as the police departed we knew what to expect and were not surprised to see the off-duty screw we had passed earlier during our drive down the hill come in to take part in the chastisement which was meted out to us in the punishment block.

I never saw or heard anything of Tommy after I left Portland. I would think that the two months spent in the punishment block probably decided his future for him. As for myself I was becoming more bitter as the months passed by.

Whenever I think of my days at Portland I only seem to remember the violence and the continual bullying that went on. Not only the staff but the inmates allowed themselves to be used and corrupted by the system. Each house had six groups and a group leader was appointed for each. In addition, a house captain, usually one of the toughest guys in the house, was also created. A new inmate would be introduced to the house captain as soon as he was allocated to a particular house. The house rules and regulations would then be spelt out by the captain and any of the group leaders who were present. The first thing that would happen to the new inmate would be the haircut, when all of his hair would be shaved off.

On my arrival, I didn't fancy my hair being shaved by another inmate. My attitude led to my first confrontation with the house captain. He decided he was going to let me know who was 'governor' straight away. However, it soon became clear to him that I wasn't just another push-over and he had to call on the help of his group leaders. I remember that not a day passed without me being involved in at least one fight, until the other inmates realized that I wasn't going to conform to their ways of running the house.

Having established this understanding I was then ignored by most of the leaders. I was later offered the job of being the next leader, which I turned down. I never wished to be used as a tool of the authorities. I suppose I could have made life a lot easier for myself if I had conformed, but I don't think it would have done anything for my mental attitude.

Just before I was due to be discharged I was called before the Governor and told that I would be given the papers appertaining to my National Service on the day of my release.

CHAPTER FIVE

'You're in the Army Now'

S o here I was, twenty years old, just released from three years of imprisonment and I was told to report immediately to 1st Battalion REME at Blandford Camp, Dorset, which I did. I wasn't very happy with the fact that I didn't get a chance to go home first, but I thought they'd let me go home once they knew that I'd not seen anyone there for three years. I might have known better.

'You're in the Army now, go and get kitted out,' I was told.

The next day, after getting our kit, we were told to assemble in the gymnasium, where we were met by a couple of guys in red and black striped jerseys who told us they were PTIs.

'Line up,' the first jersey said. 'Do we have any sportsmen here?'

Most of the recruits put their hands up and declared they'd participated in various sports. Then he said, 'You, the bloke with the funny hair cut' – Borstal style – 'can you do anything? Play football, box or run?'

'Yes, a bit of each,' I said.

'Oh, a superman, eh?' he sneered. 'Well, let's see how you are with the gloves on.'

Putting a pair on himself he then gave me a hook to the

body. That was the first and last blow he threw. All the hate and frustration came boiling out of me and I just gave him a fusillade of punches that left him flat on the floor.

He wasn't very talented himself, but I did meet one or two very good boxers while I was at Blandford and also one of the fastest fighters I ever sparred with. He was Darkie Hughes from Cardiff, who was the current ABA champion and eventually went on to fight for the professional title.

I couldn't settle into anything at this period in my life and it wasn't very long before I was going AWOL from Blandford. After a short period I was brought back to the camp to be charged with going absent and it was then that I met Mick Emmett-Dunne, the provost sergeant. He was apparently a legend in that camp and was certainly a striking-looking guy, well over six foot with a proportionate build. I was to meet Mick again several years later in Dartmoor. I was going through a pretty rough time and had to have an operation. The authorities wouldn't let me go to Freedom Fields Hospital in Plymouth, which was only fifteen miles away, and I was taken two hundred miles to London's Wormwood Scrubs Prison, where they had the facilities to operate. After my operation I was put into the ordinary wing to await a transfer back to Dartmoor. It was while I was in the hospital that I got some old papers and read that Mick, who was a professional soldier, had gone to Germany with his unit, after I had left Blandford Camp for a 'better life', and whilst there had been accused of killing another soldier with a karate blow during a row about the other soldier's wife, who was a German girl. Mick had married the girl, after the burial of her husband,

and had settled down. The coroner had apparently concluded that the guy had hanged himself but, after some pretty strong rumours, it was decided to exhume the body and Mick was eventually charged and sentenced to life imprisonment for his murder.

It was whilst I was going into church, after being put into the ordinary wing from the hospital, that I first saw Mick in the Scrubs; he was handing out the hymn books. He had his eyes cast downwards and, as I clutched the book without taking it, he looked up blankly at first then, with recognition, his eyes came alight. I was to remind him of his words to me all those years before. 'If you don't get rid of that hatred, you'll spend many years in prison.'

It was at that same time that I got another surprise. I was standing in the doorway of my cell when I saw a familiar face walking past me with a chamber pot in his hand on his way to slopping out. The last time I had seen that face was in the gym when he was training for the British light-heavyweight title. His name, George Walker, later became well known in the City with his company Brent Walker. Many great pundits of the boxing game still rate George's title fight with Dennis Powell, at the Liverpool Stadium, as the greatest light-heavyweight title fight this country has ever seen. It was sad to see him walking along that landing. He told me, later that day, that he was in for taking a lorry load out of the docks and had been given two years. It didn't seem to do him any harm, for the next time I was to meet George, years later at the Log Cabin club in Wardour Street, Soho, he was well on the way to making his first million.

I decided that there was no way I was ever going to

finish off my National Service. I'd just spent three years at Portland Borstal and then I was expected to go straight into the Army without a break. I wanted to see some of the bright lights, so when I was released from the guardroom I wasted no time. I ran off and made my way back to London. It didn't take me long to find some of my old pals and a few of the girls I knew were still working around the West End. But by then they had gone a little up-market. It wasn't the Soho cafés they frequented, but the Lyons Corner Houses. There was one in Coventry Street that everyone used in the daytime, and the one in the Strand was open all night, so that was a popular meeting place after hours. You could always expect to see certain faces in the Corner House in those days.

That is where I was to meet my first real girlfriend, Zoe 'Mickie' Progel. She was later to be nicknamed Zippy Zoe by the press as she was the first and only woman to escape over the wall of Holloway Prison. She was a great girl, full of fun, and nothing ever worried her. We went everywhere together for a while; it was like having a mate as well as a girlfriend.

But back to my life on the run from the Army. We still carried identification cards in those days, unless you were in the Army when you had your pay book. I had to be a bit careful so I'd sometimes borrow my friends' ID cards. One particular ID caused me some awkward moments as it was in the name of Angus McKenzie with an address in Glasgow. So on the odd occasion I got 'pulled' by the law for my ID card I had to adopt a Glaswegian accent. I must be the worst mimic in the world but, for some unknown reason, it was never questioned.

Years later when I was in Dartmoor I heard of a pop singer called Karl Denver. He had a few big hits in the fifties and sixties. Then I saw a photograph of him and realized that he was my old pal Angus McKenzie. I've had many a good night out with him since those days and now, by a strange coincidence, he lives just around the corner from me.

Whilst on the run from the Army I was in a very mixed-up frame of mind. My hatred for anyone in authority had built up in me since my early days in St Vincent's, but I still had my sense of fair play. Consequently I was a bit choosy about the guys I knocked around with. It was obvious to me that, having a record, I was going to have to obtain my living as a criminal, but there were certain things that I would never have done, such as pushing drugs or living off immoral earnings, and luckily I've kept to those principles throughout my life.

At the same time, there seemed to be a different atmosphere of violence creeping into the underworld at this time. Perhaps I noticed it more from having been out of circulation for a while. It was more sinister than the odd punch-up and the gang wars with a bit of razor slashing. That was a kind of accepted violence that didn't affect the ordinary public. But now we had crimes like the 'Antiquis Murder', where a gang of smash-and-grab bandits, including one of the Jenkins brothers, gunned down a motorcyclist who 'had a go' and were later hanged at Wandsworth. There were so many of these types of incidents it seemed that the ordinary criminal was getting more desperate. But the coming to London of the Messina brothers brought a whole new type of organized crime more reminiscent of the American Mafia.

The Messinas were born in Sicily but learned their trade in Malta and spread their wings to Cairo, Morocco and Spain before landing in London. They were so well organized that they were in this country for many years before the public heard of them, but anyone close to the goings on in Soho and the fringes of Mayfair knew that there was a powerful force emerging in the underworld and that it was being financed by prostitution. The Messinas had set up a vice ring that was pretty well impregnable because they had imported all of their girls from the Continent. To avoid the girls getting involved with anyone that had a natural abhorrence of 'poncing' (living off immoral earnings) they used mainly Maltese as their front men and collectors. These Maltese men would do all of the dirty work, enforcing strict rules on the girls, and seeming to enjoy all of the violence that went with the running of an organized vice ring. The Maltese heavies were allowed to open the near-beer 'clip joints' and the drinking clubs where the girls could relax when they were not working. They also ran the 'speilers' (illegal gaming clubs) that seemed to be the meeting places for all of the ponces and their cronies.

There were five Messina brothers: Eugene, Salvatore, Carmello, Alfredo and Attillio. Although people would whisper of the Messinas it wasn't until Eugene slashed one of the girls himself that their name came into the open. It was then that a newspaper man called Duncan Webb decided to expose the Messinas but he only managed to scratch the surface of their empire. Eugene got about three years' imprisonment but the publicity made the Messinas seem more dangerous and sinister, and quicker to use violence. The ordinary London gangster didn't like those who lived off immoral earnings and so there were plenty of little niggling squabbles and razor fights, which suited the local constabulary as they gave an excuse to lock up a few of the local villains. The situation came to a head when my friend Tommy Smithson put a Maltese called George Caruana in hospital. A little while after this three Maltese guys went to Tommy's flat, which he shared with Fay Richardson, and gunned him down – but not before he had stabbed one of them with a pair of scissors. One of the three Maltese, Philip Ellul, was to get a life sentence for this and he was to join me a few years later in the quarry in Dartmoor, but by now the Messinas were millionaires and were to be seen quite openly in their chauffeur-driven limos, always with a very attractive girl at their side.

The girls were allowed to ply their trade unhindered throughout Mayfair and the Old Bill that were being paid off made sure that the girls would only be pulled in now and again and quickly released on bail so that they could get straight back on the beat to cover their fine with the first client they met. The Messinas had a network of flats around Shepherds Market, tiny little bedsits with a maid, usually a retired prostitute. Since the maximum fine for prostitution was only £2, it was a very lucrative business.

Finally Duncan Webb's persistence started to pay off. He kept the Messina name in the paper as often as he could and eventually started to rattle the family. When their names were raised in Parliament Eugene fled the country and opened up in Belgium. He was later arrested for white slavery and spent six years in jail. Three of the other brothers left shortly afterwards and the only one that stayed behind was Alfredo. He carried on operating behind the scenes for many years but he was at long last arrested for living off the immoral earnings of a French girl. He was asked to explain how he had amassed a fortune in three bank accounts and had he ever worked since coming to Britain? 'No,' was the answer. He was sentenced to two years, the maximum penalty for poncing, and was deported on his release. The only other Messina I was to meet after this was Attillio, when he decided to return to England to set up in business again. He must have done well because when one of his girls, who happened to be one of the very few English prostitutes he ran, decided to get out she went to the police and Attillio was arrested in his nice suburban house. He protested his innocence but was eventually sentenced to four years' imprisonment. That was when I met him and he certainly didn't look like the type of bloke that could instill fear and violence into a whole community. He looked more like a middle-class commuter and seemed so out of place in prison that he reminded me of a scared rabbit.

But although I was aware of the Messinas when I was on the run from the Army I didn't come across them. I was looking for ways to make some easy money and hanging out in the Corner House with guys like Curly King. He was one of the nicer people I came across in those days and we got into a few scrapes together. I was also seeing a girl who I'd met before I was sent to Portland. She was very attractive, a lovely girl, but I wasn't looking for a steady relationship. However, she became pregnant and we had a son, Jeff, a beautiful boy. I thought I should try to do the responsible thing so we married in a register office and got a tiny flat together. But she hated my way of life and moved back home. I realized even then that a lot of what she said made good sense but I kept looking for ways to make my fortune. I loved her in many ways and would keep going back to her with the intention of fulfilling my responsibilities but my good intentions would never last. We had two daughters, born between prison sentences. To my everlasting regret I never got to know my children very well but I know my ex-wife was a good mother. Jeff has become a musician and my eldest daughter went to university and has done well for herself despite not having a father about.

I eventually ended up working with a team of guys that specialized in stealing lorries. In those days lorry drivers used to park their wagons up in transport café car parks and leave them overnight. There were none of the sophisticated anti-theft devices that they have now so it was simply a matter of going out and looking for the right wagon. Once found, our driver would be inside the cabin and driving it away within minutes. We used to take pot-luck in the early days, we'd just hope there was a worthwhile load, and we often got more rubbish than good gear. But we had our odd tickle, when the champagne would flow. We used to take all of our stuff to a guy in Commercial Road. Whenever we'd pull up he'd say, 'Have you hit the jackpot yet?'

Then we'd tell him we didn't know what was in it yet and he would groan. He used to say, 'Why don't you check it out first, I've still got all those tin-openers you brought me.'

What is a typical 'fence' (a buyer of stolen goods)? Well, they come in all shapes and sizes and you couldn't pick one out by looking at him, but they've all got one thing in common, and that is, they are probably the brightest of all of the criminal fraternity. People think of a fence as a guy who looks and acts like Fagin in Dickens' *Oliver Twist*. Well, they may not all look like him but most of those I've known act like him. So did Abe Tee, the man who bought thousands of tin-openers from us, and had them for a long time afterwards. He knew from experience that we were a professional team and after he'd met our driver, Jock from Kilmarnock, he knew that we would eventually come up with the goods.

Jock had just finished his National Service and there was nothing he didn't know about lorries. Whatever the size, he could handle them as though each one was a Mini Cooper (which wasn't always to our advantage, as I will relate later). We had all met through a mutual friend who had known Jock in the Army. Jock didn't want to go back to Kilmarnock until he'd made a few quid, so he was quite prepared to lend his expertise to us until he'd made enough to go back North in style. Unfortunately we were all a bit green at the beginning and the first wagons that Jock pulled away were full of rubbish; hence our man Abe giving us a reminder about the tin-openers. Mind you, he did have a problem at the time as they were a new design and he couldn't send a team of demonstrators around the markets while he was the only bloke in the whole country to have them 'in stock'.

However, we learned from our experiences and, by checking out the lorries beforehand, started to get a few sensible loads and some good 'tickles'. So Abe decided to invest in a new 'slaughter' (a place to change over and store stolen goods). He bought a small-holding in the country with a big barn, and we were taken down to familiarize ourselves with the terrain. We were a bit disappointed about the narrow country roads we would have to traverse – apart from Jock, who was overjoyed. When he saw some of the hairpin bends he couldn't wait to tackle them with a big articulated lorry.

The first disaster came not through Jock's driving but through Abe failing to test the drive into the farm yard, which was just a cinder track. With the first truck we took in Jock was told by Abe to run around to the side of the barn and then to get rid of the unit. Jock let the legs down on the trailer and went on his merry way to dump the unit on the other side of London. The rest of us went into the house to look at the delivery note and do our business with Abe. When we came out again we saw, to our horror, that the legs had sunk about two feet into the ground. We spent hours getting the stuff unloaded and then 'our man' said he was going to dismantle the trailer as he had a bloke in Oxfordshire who was going to buy the axles, wheels and other spare parts.

From then on I saw two very lucrative businesses built up, but they were not without a few headaches. The most serious of these came when Jock, who was bringing in a load of carpets, rounded a bend at about sixty miles per hour and simply turned the wagon on to its side. There were carpets everywhere and the road was completely blocked, but more seriously, it was only about half a mile from the slaughter. The only thing we could do was leave the carpets decorating the road and pick up Jock, who was a bit dazed, and drive him down to the slaughter to let our man know. There was a bit of a panic about all of the spare parts lying around in the barn which there was no time to move. But amazingly, although the Old Bill came to remove the carpets they never paid a visit to any of the premises in the area.

It was while we were waiting to see how that little episode was going to work out that Jock decided to go back to Scotland and take all of his clan on a week-long binge. They looked forward to his periodic visits as he always took a stack of money up there with him and stayed until it was all gone. When Jock returned to London we were still giving the slaughter a miss but we had a friend with a coal-yard in south London, and for a few quid we could always use it at a pinch. So Jock, who was skint again, decided to go out and do a quick bit of moonlighting. He phoned me at about 1.30 a.m. to say he had a load and could I meet him. By about 2.30 a.m. I was with him and the lorry which he had parked in a square in a quiet part of London. We opened the back and found it was loaded with apples. I looked at Jock and said with exasperation: 'Where do you think we're going to sell this lot? Why didn't you check the load first?'

Then I remembered a guy I knew who had a couple of fruit shops and rang him from a phone box. He wasn't very pleased at being woken up at 3 a.m., as he normally got up about 5 a.m. to go to the market.

'What kind of apples are they?' he asked.

'I don't know,' I said, surprised at the question. All apples were the same to me.

'Go and have a look; if they're foreign Golden Delicious I can probably place them for you,' he said.

I went back to Jock. 'Open that wagon again, I might have found a buyer,' I said.

I couldn't believe my eyes when I read on the boxes 'French Golden Delicious'.

I went back to the phone and told my man, who was delighted. I then phoned the coalman and told him I needed his yard and, as it was so late, I told him he'd get an extra few bob. We found there were 1,200 cases in the wagon and my man gave us 10/- a case for them. £600 was a pretty good earner in those days as one could have bought a house for that sort of money.

Everyone had a good day and so it was off to the West End for a day out, the coalman, the fruiterer, Jock and I.

We had some pretty good days to follow that one and things seemed to go without too many hiccups until the Old Bill decided to do something about our little enterprise. We were surrounded just as we were about to drive a lorry away from a yard in Hertfordshire. Three of us were sent to Hertfordshire Assizes where Mr Justice Croom-Johnson gave us five years' imprisonment each.

CHAPTER SIX

The Cat-O'-Nine-Tails Scars for Ever

I was taken to Pentonville to start my sentence. From the moment I stepped inside the prison I knew it was going to start all over again, the same as Wormwood Scrubs, same as Portland. There was a reception committee of six screws waiting for me. Eyeing the group of new inmates the spokesman demanded: 'Which one is Mason?'

'Me,' I replied.

'Right, come with us.'

I was taken straight to the punishment block and told, 'This is where you'll do all your bird if you once get out of line. We've checked your record out and we don't like people like you. The Governor will see you tomorrow.'

The same old intimidation routine. I thought, I'm not going to have five years of this, and I told them so. I also told every one of them that if anyone laid a finger on me I would eventually do the same to him. Then it started.

On my first day in the mailbag shop, where there was a 'no talking' rule, one of the discipline screws suddenly said to me: 'Stop talking or you'll be put on report.' As I hadn't opened my mouth I knew that this was a confrontation and I knew that I could not stop what was going to happen. So

I just swore at him and said: 'Get on with what you've got in mind.'

He made a signal to the screw in the observation box, who promptly rang the alarm bell. Almost immediately, as if they had been waiting outside, the door of the workshop was flung open and the heavy mob came flooding in – about a dozen of them. The discipline screw pointed at me and declared: 'He threatened me.' Seconds later I was being dragged to the door, struggling and lashing out as best as I could. The other cons started to boo the screws and it seemed that an eruption of violence was just a knife-edge away. Then we were through the door, which slammed shut behind us. Out of sight of the cons, the screws seemed to go mad. Screaming 'He tried to start a riot' they began smashing me with their batons while I tried vainly to protect myself.

It came as no surprise when, following this incident, I was charged with an unprovoked attack on a screw. After a couple of months in the punishment block on a bread and water diet and loss of a few months' remission, I was sent to Wandsworth, where I believe they thought they would be better equipped for dealing with someone that wouldn't lie down to them. They were certainly better equipped, but I still wasn't going to give in. I spent the next year in and out of the punishment block – more in than out.

By this time I was going through plenty of aggravation with the authorities. The Governor of Wandsworth at that time was a man called Lawton. He was the harshest, most pitiless person I ever met in my life. I think the day he presided over me being flogged with the cat-o'-nine-tails was the happiest day of his life, but I can tell you that one of the unhappiest days for him was the day I humiliated him in the brush shop.

During one of my breaks from the punishment cells I was determined to get one over him for what he'd put me through over the past few months. I put a bucket into the toilet and told everyone that I knew to use it. They started to go one after the other – the discipline screws must have thought there was something in the food with so many cons needing to use the toilet.

After about a dozen blokes had used the bucket it wasn't a pretty sight and it stank to high heaven. Lawton, as regular as clockwork, came through that shop at about 11 a.m. along with his henchman. He had all of the screws terrified of him; as soon as he walked in they would all leap to attention and salute and shout, 'All correct, sir.' He loved it, the pompous little sod. But I soon took the sneer off his face when I dumped the contents of the bucket over his head and threw the residue over his henchman, who had the grace to vomit. I got a terrible beating for that, but it was worth it and also gave an extra lightness to the whole atmosphere in the prison for quite some time.

I was to have one or two more run-ins with the prison staff which resulted in me spending more time in the strongbox. When I came out of the punishment block I was put into D Wing and given a job in the tailor's shop, although I was still supposed to sew mailbags. Only the privileged few did any tailoring and that was restricted to making prisoners' shirts. It wasn't unusual to get a shirt that had one sleeve six inches longer than the other, or a collar that joined somewhere beneath one's ear. As soon as

I got into the workshop I knew there would be trouble as the discipline screw sitting with the alarm bell at his elbow was an old enemy of mine. He never took his eyes off me from the minute I got in the shop as we both knew that he'd been in on a few of the kickings I had received whilst in the punishment block. If the struggle was to go on I had to beat him.

When the dinner break came at noon we were 'rubbed down' (searched) and sent back into our cells. Then I realized why I'd been put into the tailor's shop. It was because the workshop was right next to the wing I was in and also adjacent to the punishment block. They were ready for me. I had my suspicions confirmed when I came out into the exercise yard after dinner. There was the discipline screw talking to another officer who was supposed to be their hard man, and they were giving me the once over. I noticed there were more screws on duty than usual. I knew then that they had taken me seriously when, lying in a pool of blood in the strongbox, I warned them I would be back at them. As I walked into the workshop that afternoon I made up my mind that I was going to 'do' the discipline screw no matter what the consequences were. I sat on my stool and glanced casually around. I saw that he had been joined in the shop by three fellow screws. I knew it wasn't going to be easy but I also knew that this was the time for confrontation and I had to do it. I stood up and said, looking straight at him, 'I'm going for a shit.'

'Sit down. You don't do anything without permission,' he said.

But by this time I was up close to him and his momentary hesitation was all I needed. I leaped on to his high seat and hooked him to the chin, then dragged him out of the box and with a quick fusillade of punches flattened him. I looked around to see their hard man bearing down on me but I could read the fear in his eyes and as he reached out to grab me, I moved inside and 'nutted' him. He went down as if poleaxed and his massive frame was cringed away, trying to cover up. The other two were just rooted to the floor but I saw the Principal Officer in his office with the old-fashioned telephone to his ear. I dived in, took the phone from him and hit him on the head with it. He just rolled up like a ball in the corner of the office. I ran quickly back towards the door and noticed that one of the other discipline screws was ringing the alarm bell. I knew I didn't have a lot of time, as it was guaranteed that the heavy mob would be waiting for the bell to ring. I started to grab the sewing machines and throw them in front of the door. I heard Wally Probyn say ruefully, 'Fuck me! I've waited nine months to get this machine, now look at it.'

But I was too late. In no time at all the screws were crashing the door in and were swarming all over me. They hauled me through the door and threw me down the steps leading into D Wing. I was back on my feet before they could reach me and was able to get inside the door, 'nutted' the screw in the doorway and grabbed his stick and started to belt the others as they came in. But I couldn't hold out for long; I was soon forced to the floor with ten or a dozen sticks thudding down on me. They then proceeded to beat me the length of D Wing, over the centre and down into the punishment block. The screws dragging me along deliberately smashed my head against the iron stanchions holding up the landing above.

By the time I arrived at the strongbox I was barely conscious. The last thing I remember was a screw jumping on me while the baton wielders were beating my testicles. I was beyond fighting back – all I could do was try to protect my body from the worst of their attacks. Eventually I must have passed out.

I woke up in the strongbox strapped into a body belt. It felt as though every bone in my body was broken. My mouth was full of blood, the same blood that covered my whole body. In the dim light I could make out that I had no clothes on. I must have lain like that for hours – I was freezing cold and the pain was almost unbearable. At that point I was beyond caring whether I lived or died.

Eventually the door was thrown open and half a dozen screws came in with one of the doctors who started to say, 'Oh, so you can't take it yourself, eh? You've sent for the doctor.'

'Fuck off! I don't need you,' I snarled back, and with that he lashed me around the face with his stethoscope.

The next morning, this would be about sixteen hours later, the screws came in and dragged me to the strongbox next door while the cleaner came down to clean up the blood. I was still caked in it and could hardly move when they told me to stand for adjudication. I just spat the blood out of my mouth as the Governor arrived with the Chief and stood in the doorway looking down at me as I lay naked on the floor.

'What's the charge?' asked the Governor.

'Gross personal violence to members of the staff, sir,' came the reply.

'What are the details?' the Governor demanded.

'Unprovoked attack on five members of the staff. He had to be restrained with the minimum amount of force,' answered the screw.

'Right, he'll be remanded for the visiting magistrates,' the Governor replied.

Then off they went leaving me lying there. Later that day they came in with a bucket of water and washed me down like an animal, then dragged me back into the first cell I'd been in while their creepy cleaner cleaned up the other one. I knew that I had broken bones in my hands and I had a severe pain in the lower part of my body and back which took many months to subside.

After two days with nothing to eat they finally brought a mess of goulash on a papier mâché plate and a cup of prison tea. My hands were still cuffed in the body belt so I couldn't use them. Instead I was forced to eat from the plate off the floor like an animal. I realized that one of my teeth had broken off in my gum when I went to pick the cup up with my teeth to tilt it. Although feeling more than a little depressed I was also more determined than ever that I was going to beat them.

For about two weeks, I was not allowed any access to a toilet and not being able to use my hands had to perform my bodily functions where I was. The screws dragged me from cell to cell, their cleaner following to clean up after me.

Eventually, eight screws came into the strongbox with a pair of slippers, trousers and a jacket about two sizes too big for me. They pulled the trousers on me and tied them round with a piece of mailbag rope, then wrapped the jacket right around me, buttoned it up and said, 'Visiting magistrates'.

Everyone was locked in their own cells while I was taken to the boardroom. They didn't seem to mind the magistrates seeing me but they didn't want the other cons to witness my condition. The trial was farcical like they always were – typical kangaroo courts. The screws gave their evidence then I was asked why I had attacked these officers.

'You know already that these people have been treating me with violence for years, trying to make me submit, for their own perverse reasons,' I said bitterly. 'You're part of the same system, you won't listen to anything I say. You're not interested in investigating anything. You've only got to look at me to see what I'm going through. Are you going to investigate what's going on in here?' I demanded.

With that the Chairman said, 'Take him outside.' After about five minutes I was taken back into the boardroom and told by the Chairman, 'Your punishment has been sent for recommendation to the Home Office.'

I was taken back to the punishment block and put into one of the ordinary cells, still bare of furniture but with a log set in the floor to sit on. I could hear the other cons shouting to each other through the windows of the punishment cells. I heard my name being called, but it was a bit difficult to pull myself up to a window for any length of time as I still had a couple of breaks in my hands. I heard that Teddy Gibbs, Johnny Cotton and Slash Waters were in the punishment block. Ted was next door to me and he had been flogged in the past for whacking a screw in the face with a brick. So when he heard that my punishment had been referred to the Home Office he said, 'You'll be getting corporal punishment. In about two weeks' time, the doctor will come to give you a medical, then if he asks you to take your shirt off and looks at your back, you'll be given the cat-o'-nine-tails, but if you have to take your strides off and he looks at your arse, you'll be getting the birch.'

Subsequently, about two weeks later, the medical screw came in with the heavy mob and asked me to piss in a bottle.

'Fuck off, I'm not co-operating,' I told him.

They just laughed and walked out. Next came the body-belt brigade who put the body belt on me. This was the quack's idea as he had to use the stethoscope for its proper function and he didn't fancy getting a whack himself this time. After he'd gone they left me alone until the next day. At midday, after everyone had been fed except me, the door was thrown open and about twelve screws stood outside.

'Take this prisoner to the laundry,' the Chief said. When I got to the laundry there stood the Governor and the doctor with their henchmen. The Governor wasted no time.

'The Home Office has confirmed your punishment. You will receive twelve strokes of the cat-o'-nine-tails and loss of six months' remission. Remove the prisoner's upper clothing and proceed to the frame.'

I was taken to the back section of the laundry. There stood a large wooden frame in the shape of a triangle. Next to this frame was an ordinary wooden table. On the table I saw firstly a large square of lint smeared with ointment, then a large canvas belt which I discovered was to protect my kidneys, a collar of soft material to protect my neck, and a long rectangular box which presumably held the cat-o'-nine-tails.

I had just taken all this in when my ankles were shackled to the legs of the frame and my wrists cuffed to two pulleys. My head was pushed through a slit in the canvas sheet attached to the frame and a cover was buckled over my head to stop me looking around to see who was flogging me. There was another canvas sheet attached to the left side of my frame to stop me seeing that side. The pulleys were then pulled by two screws who took pains to avoid looking at me – perhaps they were squeamish. I could look to my right side where my 'friend' the doctor stood so that he could see both my face and back.

I heard the footsteps of the screw who was to administer the punishment. He came to the table. I could hear him open the box and take the whip out of it and I could hear the swish of the strands as he sorted them out. It seemed as though everyone was holding their breath, it was so quiet. I started to think about what Gibbsy had said to me, when he knew I was going to have the 'pussy': 'The first one hurts so much that it numbs your back and after that you can hardly feel anything.' It was some comfort.

So there I was in this atmosphere of silence and hatred, helpless and despairing because of my own frustration. I knew I had to take my punishment without a murmur to help me through my own private war against the system.

When the first stroke came it hurt a fair bit, but having steeled myself for the anticipated pain I was able to stand it pretty well. The Governor counted 'One' and in the quiet I again heard the screw sorting out the strands of the whip.

The next stroke came but this time it was twice as bad. It seemed to land right in the same place as the first, as did the rest of the strokes and they seemed to get progressively harder, slicing into my bruised skin. The Governor counted slowly as the sweat poured down my face. It probably only took about twenty minutes but it seemed never-ending. It was only after they released me from the frame that my back started to go numb and I realized that Gibbsy had got his time scale entirely wrong.

It wasn't till I got back to the cell that the numbness started to go, replaced by a real shocking deep throbbing that was getting progressively more painful. I knew that the screws were looking through the spy-hole to see my reaction, which steeled me against showing any emotion. I felt what I thought was sweat running down my body under my arm, but when I looked it was blood. I looked at the right side of my chest and I could see where one of the strokes had cut deep into my flesh. That was the closest I ever came to giving in. Thank God I did not know, then, that this was just the beginning.

CHAPTER SEVEN

The Condemned, the Mad Axeman and Jack the Hat

The first few day after having the cat-o'-nine-tails were a strange time for me. I was still recovering from the beating I had taken and my back was extremely sore. It was a few weeks before I could lie on it properly and when I went back to the workshop I had a few well-meaning mates come to welcome me back from the punishment block and, without thinking, give me a slap on the back. Then the screw who had to rub down everyone as they returned to the wing after work nearly had a heart attack when I screamed at him to take his hands off me.

The atmosphere in Wandsworth was tense and getting worse. Of the 1,500 or so men there only a handful were fighting back, either physically or by trying to smuggle word out of what was happening within the prison. But when news got around that someone was being beaten in the punishment block, all the cons showed their solidarity in the only way they could. I'll never forget the menacing, awesome sound of over a thousand prisoners banging their pots and plates on the metal-clad doors and chanting for the blood of the people who had been tormenting them for years. What with the brutality in the punishment block, and the number of hangings in Wandsworth at that time, the prison was like a cauldron waiting to boil over.

The condemned cells, which always seemed to be occupied, were right above the punishment block and at the opposite end to the strongbox. When you had finished the first part of your sentence you were moved from the strongbox to the other end of the block to finish off your 'confined to cell' bit, commonly known as CC. So it turned out that over the various times I was in Wandsworth I was often unfortunate enough to be located underneath the condemned cell and adjacent to the cell the body would drop into. I hated the moment when, on the day before an execution, the hangman came into the prison and, while the condemned man was on exercise, tested the trap door. It dropped with a dreadful sound of finality that reverberated around the wing.

Some hangings affected us more than others. There was a guy called Whiteway who must have been a complete lunatic. He was the infamous tow-path murderer and he thought he was Tarzan. He used to do the Tarzan call frequently, and everyone would shout, 'Hurry up and hang the bastard.'

Then there was a guy called Burgess. I think he did a murder in a hotel in Croydon. I remember him because he was very quiet for the three weeks he was waiting to hang, but on the morning he was due to 'go' he cracked and set about the two screws who were with him in the condemned cell. I could hear the thuds and shouts above me and the insistent ringing of the alarm bell. Then I heard the heavy mob arrive and the beating seemed to go on for ages, with the condemned man screaming his head off. After some time everything went quiet and they came to take us for our exercise. When we came back from the yard I saw a pile of clothes outside the PO's office. They were all ripped and covered in blood. I knew they had belonged to Burgess as they had no buttons on, only tapes to keep them together.

But the incident that upset the whole prison more than any other was the hanging of Derek Bentley. Derek, who was eighteen at the time, had been sentenced to death for being with a chap called Chris Craig when the latter shot a policeman, notwithstanding the fact that Bentley was already in police custody when Craig shot the copper. Arguments have gone on for many years about whether he was guilty or not. Like many people I believe it was a revenge execution because the boy, Chris Craig who did the actual murder, was legally too young to hang. The evidence against Bentley, that he told Craig to 'Let him have it', was interpreted as an instruction to shoot the policeman when he could have meant that Craig should hand over the gun. In fact there is now even some doubt about whether Bentley said those words at all.

I was right under his cell for the whole of the time he was waiting to be hanged, and I used to look out of the window each day and see his mother and sister come to the back of the condemned cell and climb the iron staircase into the cell next to it to visit him. They both seemed to age so much in the space of a few weeks. It was terrible to see, because they, like many people, believed he was innocent of any murder. We all thought Bentley was certain to get a reprieve and they must have kidded him right up to the last minute. The day before his execution I watched the hangman, who on this occasion was Pierrepoint's assistant Harry Allen, come down the path with a big grin on his face to test the trap-door. In some ways he looked more sinister dressed in his everyday bowler hat and dark suit than Pierrepoint himself did in his trilby. They had taken Bentley for his exercise at the side of the hospital while they tried the trap-door, which banged down into the cell next to mine and shook the dividing wall. I was in that cell many a time when people were hanged but I still have very clear memories of Derek Bentley playing a tune on a comb and a piece of toilet paper the night before he died. There was a very strained atmosphere created that day in Wandsworth, and it was a long time before it lifted.

It was while in Wandsworth at about this time that I first met Jack 'the Hat' McVitie and Frank Mitchell, 'The Mad Axeman'. Frank had gone to Portland after I'd left and I often heard stories about this young man there with super-human strength who was always championing the little and weak guys. When I met him I understood why he impressed people so much. He was very good-looking and a perfect physical specimen, about six foot two inches in height and weighing about sixteen stone – all of which was muscle. He was probably the strongest man I ever met and he would exercise at every opportunity. His presence in the prison reassured quite a lot of men as he was against all kinds of bullying. Although he has been nicknamed 'The Mad Axeman' he was never mad and would never have hit anyone with an axe. He was a victim of the system: a big, gentle giant who hated to see people weaker than himself being treated like dirt.

Frank also loved a good laugh. Being a fitness fanatic he used to do a couple of hundred press-ups and sit-ups every day. Once most of his problems in prison had been sorted out Frank was left mostly to his own devices – until the arrival of a new, zealous Chief Officer. Frank had found a very thick manhole cover, the type with concrete and steel, which he used as a weight to build up his body. He had no problem pressing it over his head twenty or thirty times. The new Chief Officer, walking round the yard, saw the manhole cover lying on the ground. He asked the screw walking with him, 'What's that doing there?'

'That's Mitchell's training weight,' said the screw.

The new Chief had obviously been filled in about Frank, but for some reason he decided to test the water himself.

'I want this object removed to the building yard,' he ordered.

The screw bent down but he couldn't budge it. Looking sheepishly at his Chief he said, 'It's too heavy, sir.'

'Well go and get some help,' yelled the Chief.

It took the screw some time before he found a volunteer willing to give him a hand, as it seemed that no one fancied going down to the yard to take Frank's weight away, especially as the exercise period was about to start. Sure enough, just as the two screws were struggling towards the building yard with the manhole cover, Frank came out of the wing.

'What are you doing with my weight?' he asked quite mildly.

'It's not our fault, Frank, the new Chief ordered us to take it away.'

With this Frank took it from them and, with absolutely no effort whatsoever, strolled back to the end of the yard. Over his shoulder he said, 'You'd better tell the Chief to come and get it himself.' Then as Frank started to smile the whole prison yard fell about laughing. I believe the prison Governor must have had a word with the Chief as from then on whenever he passed Frank he used to say, 'Good morning, Mitchell. How's the training going?'

Although outwardly tough Frank was very kind-hearted, as his actions showed. He never smoked and in the later days of his sentence, when he was allowed to buy sweets or tobacco with his earnings, he would send the money instead to under-privileged kids. He was a very good friend to me and I will always cherish his memory.

Jack McVitie was a different guy to Frank. He was above average height with a thick mop of black hair (which fell out later in life and he took to always wearing a hat even in a night club or restaurant). He had piercing blue eyes that always seemed to be laughing. There were many times when he and I were recovering from a beating and I'd look at Jack who, with a twinkle in his eye, would remark something like, 'I'll be all right when I get out of here, some birds like guys with battered features.'

Jack had been what they termed a 'Borstal failure', which meant that they couldn't beat him into submission, so he was sent to the punishment block in Reading Prison. That's where I first started to hear about him and I knew he had to be a bit special because there were quite a few blokes in those days who were not taking it lying down. Although I got to know many such men as the years went by, my friendship with Frank and Jack was very close. During one period, when we were all out of the punishment block, we managed to snatch a few words together. We knew that the prison staff at Wandsworth were determined to break us and we decided that if we were to have any chance we'd stick together as much as we could so if one was taken to the punishment block the other two would follow.

For instance, one afternoon I was working in the brush shop. Among the screws in the shop that day was a member of the Wandsworth heavy mob. He was always boasting about his prowess as a 'hard man', but he would forget to mention that he never had less than half a dozen other screws with him when he beat a prisoner up. He used to strut around the workshop being sarcastic and generally making one's life a misery.

He had already told me that he was going to have his eyes on me and at the first chance I gave him he would break me. One day he obviously decided that the time had come to see how much I had left in me. I asked permission to go to the toilet, which we had to do. But he kept letting other people go in front of me – the usual sort of petty behaviour that eventually drives you to the end of your tether. I'd had enough so I got up to walk to the toilet. He signalled to the screw in the box to ring the alarm bell, and took my arm to guide me away, knowing full well that the heavy mob were racing to the workshop.

'Just try something and you're dead,' he said, goading me.

Something inside me snapped and I lost control, flattening him and the two other screws. By the time reinforcements arrived the three officers had barricaded themselves in the storeroom but there was no escape for me.

I was subsequently dragged and beaten back to the punishment block and into one of the two strongboxes which were in E Wing. I had been there for about two hours, feeling a bit sore, when I heard the sound of a beating going on in the next strongbox, then the door banging to. Then Frank's voice called my name. I let him know that I could hear him.

'I heard they'd done you again. Don't worry, we'll win in the end. I've done a few in the centre,' he said.

Frank had come in from the pouch shop, learnt that I'd had trouble, and run down to my cell. Seeing that it was empty, he went straight back to the centre where all the senior staff were assembled and demanded to see me. They tried to get rid of him but he stood his ground. They tried to jump him but he was too strong for them. He put four or five of them down before, by sheer weight of numbers, they overpowered him and got him into the strongbox next to mine.

The next morning, just before adjudication, we could hear the usual sounds of the heavy mob and their batons going to town and the unmistakable voice of Jack McVitie, shouting our names and saying, 'Stick together and we'll beat these bastards yet!'

It's a great feeling to know that you've got people who will stick with you even though the odds make it nearly impossible to win. I tried to express how I felt in a letter to Frank and Jack. In fact it was written on a long piece of toilet paper – which was the usual way of passing messages. We used to call these notes 'stiffs'. Jack, Frank and I would send a couple of 'stiffs' to each other every week. Frank would write about his little sister Linda who he thought the world of. He told me that he worried about her so much it would kill him if anything happened to her. Jack would go on about the screws, who he hated even more than I did, but he would also write reams about his girlfriend Anne who he loved very much and later married.

It was nearly a year before we were to come out of the punishment block, only to be split up. Frank went to Parkhurst. I don't remember where Jack went, but I was to meet them both again years later. I was told that I was going to Dartmoor and was moved over to Pentonville, to await the national draft that went to the 'Moor every month.

CHAPTER EIGHT

Dartmoor – Dark, Damp and Dank

D artmoor was commonly regarded as one of the world's grimmest prisons, housing some of Britain's most violent and notorious villains. Entering, you felt that, beneath the surface, was a smouldering fire of hatred waiting to explode into a terrible conflict that would be impossible to stop if it ever started. In my view the prison authorities had created their own dilemma by persistently sending to Dartmoor anyone who had been violent in any other prison. A prisoner needed only one other qualification – to be doing a sentence of five years or more. The man in question could turn out to be a homicidal maniac, a psychopath or just another one of those prisoners who had taken enough knocks and had decided to fight back.

There was an induction of new prisoners each month, all of whom would be collected from Pentonville Prison in London the day before they were taken to the 'Moor. They would come from Horfield in Bristol, Winson Green in Birmingham, Walton in Liverpool, Strangeways in Manchester and Armley in Leeds. But you could guarantee one thing: each of these men, wherever they came from, would be the toughest nuts from their respective towns. However, once inside Dartmoor you were not a Geordie or a Scouse or Cockney or anything else; it was a 'them and us' situation. By the time I arrived in Dartmoor I had already been on many charges for attacking prison staff and my fight with the authorities had been going on for quite some time. Now I was only one amongst many who had decided to fight back against what we perceived to be a brutal regime, so we were all treated alike.

We were taken in chains and under heavy guard to Paddington Station. After arriving at Tavistock we boarded a coach to Princetown where we immediately started to feel the gloom – the place always seemed to be shrouded in a damp, cold mist. We were driven through the gates with their inscription in French. Referring to the French prisoners of war who were first housed in Dartmoor, the inscription read: 'Pity the Vanquished'. I was not to see pity for anything for many years.

The coach drove directly to the punishment block which looked and smelled mediaeval, and dank. We were each placed in a cell where all of our kit was already deposited and told to put our own property in a brown cardboard box. The first thing that new arrivals noticed was not the cold, but the damp. Your bedding was damp, the walls were damp and even had moss growing on them. It was a grim feeling to know that you had years of this. The attitude of the screws showed that they had the situation pretty well taped and that it was going to be a hard struggle just to keep one's sanity.

The next morning we each saw the Governor who spoke to us through bars, just like a cage in the zoo, but I suppose he thought we were the animals. It was then decided which wing each of us would be allocated to and what job we were to be given. I was sent to D1 and given a job on the quarry. There were A1, A2, B1, B2, D1 and D2 wings but no C Wing as that had been destroyed during the mutiny in the 1930s. One of the leaders of that mutiny, who was to become a good friend years later, was called 'Ruby' Sparkes. He was a great character who ended up as a publican in north London. The Home Secretary has declared in Parliament that as a result of the Strangeways riot the government is going to bring in a charge of mutiny as a 'new' deterrent. They have been charging people for mutiny in British prisons before he or his father were born. They have got to do a lot more constructive talking and thinking, followed by effective action, before they stop people cracking up in our present system. There is a worryingly high suicide rate in British prisons. 'Where there is life there is hope', but some people can never see any hope for themselves and consequently are driven to extremes.

My first day on the quarry brought back dark memories. As soon as I saw it I was immediately reminded of my days at Portland on the dreaded Burma Road. A typical day's routine went as follows. We were first lined up on the tally point, counted and then taken to a gate at the back end of the prison. Two large doors were opened and as we went through them we were met by the pony patrol, who were armed with shotguns. We were then marched past the American Prisoners of War graveyard, up a steep hill until we came to a tunnel under the road that led us into the quarry proper. As we walked the biting wind would hit us, freezing our faces and hands until they were so numb with

88

the cold you could stick a needle in them without feeling it. By the time we got into the quarry proper we were already feeling pretty miserable!

As new blokes we were taken to a shed next to the stone crusher and given a 14lb hammer and told by the wizened old quarry master he would show us how to break rocks. I thought all you had to do was whack them, but I was soon to find out it wasn't as easy as that, and I was shown that rocks had a grain to them. Our job was to break the rocks that had been blown from the cliff face at the weekend, smashing them into handy sizes to be thrown into a bogie. When it was filled, the rocks would go down to the crusher to be made small enough for road chippings and breeze blocks. We were watched all the time by a screw in the gun turret near the entrance to the quarry and from a sentry box above us.

I was lucky to have three good friends among the fifty or so cons who were working in the quarry. Benny Stewart and Willie O'Dare were two Glaswegians who had been among the leaders of one of the most violent riots that had ever erupted in Wandsworth Prison. Benny and Willie were two of the last five who had held out in a store room until they were finally forced out by the screws, and their hatred for the authorities was etched in their faces. The third of the trio was Ronnie Everett, who was a giant of a man and one of the most respected people in the prison. He was quiet and intelligent but everyone knew that he was someone you didn't mess around with. He is currently in 'exile' on Spain's Costa del Sol, wanted for questioning about his alleged involvement in a £6 million robbery from Security Express. Our little quartet got on with our time in our own way and any contraband that was obtained was split equally among the four of us.

There was a small spring of the most delicious cold water about fifty yards from where we worked, and each day one of us would take time to go and fill an old dinner can from the spring. The screws would turn a blind eye when we did this but if some other poor sod, who was just doing his time, did the same thing he would find himself on report for leaving his place of work without permission. It was whilst one of us was getting the water that the wild strawberry bush was discovered. We were as excited as if we had found gold. There was the bush just above our heads, growing amongst the craggy rocks. On the bush were twelve small strawberries, not quite ripe enough for eating. We decided we would wait until they were fully ripe before having a feast as three strawberries each was a treat to look forward to. Every morning when we arrived at the quarry we would collect our hammers then make straight for the strawberry bush on the way to the rock face. It became something of a pilgrimage. Each day we would see that the strawberries were ripening and we would discuss how long we should leave them once they had turned completely red.

Then one morning, to our horror, when we turned up at the bush there were the strawberries looking healthy and nearly ripe – but two were missing. We counted them over and over again but there was no mistake. We all started to look at each other with suspicion and trudged on to work with not a word said between us. There was a very strained atmosphere all day and rocks were being smashed with more venom than usual. It seemed that everyone in the quarry sensed there was something wrong as there was a strange silence only broken by the ringing of hammers on rock.

The next morning, the day we should have been picking our strawberries, we made our way without speaking towards the bush. I heard Ronnie mutter under his breath, 'I don't believe it. Is someone mucking about?'

We all looked. Two more strawberries had gone. By now we were openly glaring at each other. Willie O'Dare was the first to crack. He said excitedly, 'Don't look at me, I've not nicked the fucking strawberries, I've only been out of sight of everyone when I've used the khazi. I've not been near the fucking bush.'

And then Benny asked, 'Who got the water yesterday?'

I had and all three stared hard at me, though no open accusations were made. I knew I hadn't done it and said so. It then became a case of if we can't trust each other, who can we trust? It soon became apparent that there was some very bad feeling building up between us and all of the other cons started to work further along the rock face, isolating us in case something terrible happened.

Just when we were on the verge of explosion Willie suddenly shouted 'Look!' and pointed to the bush. We all turned to see a blackbird pecking away at a strawberry. Instantly we felt the tension lift and started to smile at each other while a low murmuring of relieved conversation began going around the quarry. Even the screw in the gun turret came out to banter with the screw below. We all swore our great friendship with each other and then went over to pick a strawberry each, leaving two on the bush for the bird.

There was always something going on in the quarry, no

two days were alike. You would think that such a humdrum job as breaking rocks under the glare of some sadistic gaoler would be the most dreaded of tasks, but it is amazing how resilient the human body and mind can be. Some guys, my friend Mixie Walsh among them, couldn't wait to get the hammer into their hands and smash rocks. It seemed as if they were purging themselves of all the hatred that had built up inside. Then there were the little survivors who always managed to get enough rocks together to fill the bogie that took their quota to the crushing machine. Another group were the moaners, who were always writing petitions to the Home Office about how their health was deteriorating – though even they must have realized that those petitions never found their destination. The answer was always the same: 'The Home Secretary has looked into your complaint and can find no grounds to take any action.' But the fact that they had written seemed to sustain them through their ordeal. The ones we gave a wide berth to were the silent brooders who no one could get to the bottom of. Now and again they would crack up and try to attack everyone within reach. Even that was a welcome break in the monotony of our routine.

And there were the animal lovers who would collect anything from insects and mice to the odd rabbit that had strayed into the quarry. The guy with the most status amongst this group had actually hatched a jackdaw under his own armpit. The bird survived and would go everywhere with him. It was uncanny the way the bird, which was left on the window ledge when this guy went out to work, would quickly fly to the quarry, find him and land on his head or shoulder. Dartmoor had more than its fair share of jackdaws. They woke us up in the morning with their racket as they fought over the pieces of bread some cons left on the window ledges.

Most cons would, at some time, leave a scrap of hard bread outside for the birds but one night after doing so I had the most shocking experience. There were hundreds of wild ponies on Dartmoor and in the hard bleak winters many would descend from the moor into Princetown scavenging for food. They would knock the dustbins over in the screws' quarters and eat anything that was chewable. The main wall around the prison, which had been built a couple of hundred years before, would occasionally disintegrate in large sections and a big hole would appear. On one such occasion I was lying on my bed asleep when there was a terrible clattering against the window. I woke up to see the head of a pony staring at me through the window. He had come through a hole in the wall and had been around all of the window ledges collecting scraps of bread. When the doors opened in the morning all the cons were whispering to each other about the shock they got being awakened in the middle of the night by a pony knocking on the window.

One of the most amusing incidents that ever happened on the quarry whilst I was working there was Dillon's great escape. Dillon was about six and a half feet tall and built like a rugby player. But because we did not have a high opinion of his intelligence the boys started to ask him about his plan.

'I'm going to go up the rock face and disappear over the top and if the screw at the top tries to stop me I'm just going to knock him out and make a dash for it,' he replied.

'Why don't you make a dash before you come into the

quarry? It will save you the time of climbing the rock face,' we suggested sensibly.

'No, I've got a plan to hide somewhere where they'll never find me until the three-day search is over. Then I'll make my way at night to freedom,' he replied.

This was a reference to the three days when the police would block the roads leading from the prison, leaving the hazards of the moor itself to ensure that no one got away.

Now the day before Dillon was planning to escape happened to be the day we got our meat ration. Everyone would get a slice of beef with their lunch – a treat which we all looked forward to. So when Dillon asked us to give him some morsel of food to sustain him whilst he spent the days hiding on the moors, we all reluctantly decided to bring our meagre slice of meat folded inside a cob of bread. We tightened our belts and handed over our offerings to Dillon, who stuffed them into his shirt.

When the time came for Dillon to go everyone set about trying to distract the screws. One of our group went for water to the spring and another team rolled the bogie down to the crushing shed. Meanwhile a couple of the guys tried to use the toilet at the same time and distracted the screw who was telling one of them to get back to where he was working until the other one had finished. In the mean time, Dillon was proceeding up the rock face. It only took him a couple of minutes to climb to the top and over but even so it was incredible that not one of the screws noticed him. Yet every con in the quarry watched his every move as he disappeared over the top. It seemed as if the sun had come out as everyone had a smile on his face and the rocks were getting cracked with extra application. We realized that

Dillon had a two-hour start and that if he made tracks he could be beyond the area of the road blocks before he was reported missing.

About an hour later the pony patrol screw came into the quarry and asked the screw in charge, 'Is everything all right?'

'Yes, fifty-eight and all correct, sir,' the other screw replied.

'Are you sure you've got fifty-eight prisoners?' the pony screw enquired.

'Yes, sir,' came the confident reply.

'Well, you'd better count them! We've got one of yours in the punishment block. We found him sitting outside the front gate eating meat rolls,' the pony screw said.

No one will ever know what went through all of the cons' minds. But most were pretty upset about the fact that they'd missed the best meal of the week for some guy who had no intention of escaping.

I was soon to find out that nearly everyone in Dartmoor Prison carried a knife or some concealed weapon. I never felt that I needed one and certainly would not have used it so why carry it? But many did, for protection rather than because they wanted to start a fight. And of course the carrying of weapons meant that any fight was more likely to have lethal consequences, as I found out. It wasn't long after I arrived at Dartmoor that I got involved with a guy who was doing twelve years for cutting off a bloke's hand. He had a big reputation and I was known to have a reputation as well. He considered he was number one and so he didn't like it when I pulled him up for talking to a screw. Things just developed from there and we had a fight during which I knocked him out. The immediate cause was not really important, we would have had to have fought at some time because that was the way things worked.

Of course he was out for revenge but he made the mistake of telling people he was going to kill me and even saying when and where. There was a shed in the quarry, out of sight of the gun turret, where we could wash our hands and that was where he was going to get me. The day after I'd heard this I left the rock face and casually strolled in the direction of the shed, as if I was going to the toilet. Once the building hid me from view I quickly dropped behind the wall of the lean-to. I saw my attacker approaching, pulling out a twelve-inch knife as he got to the shed door. I picked up a coupling pin that was lying on the floor and hit him on the shoulder with it. He dropped the knife but before he could make another move I hit him over the head, leaving him unconscious on the floor. I threw the coupling pin in some nearby water and was back with my team on the rock face before anyone saw me. Even 'so, I was charged with attempted murder and tried at Winchester Assizes where I was found not guilty and sent back to Dartmoor.

This sort of incident was happening all the time and as I started to get to know a lot of the notorious people who were in the prison I realized we were sitting on a powder keg waiting to explode. The quietest prisoners seemed to be the 'lifers' but one soon realized that, in those days, the real killers were hanged. So the only 'lifers' then were domestic lifers or ones that had good mitigating circumstances and were therefore reprieved. Donald Hume was tried for the murder of Stanley Setty and found not guilty of murder but guilty of being an accessory. He was sentenced to twelve years for that. When he came out he told the press how he'd killed Setty then cut up his body and dropped it from a plane after an argument over money for gun-running escapades in the Middle East. He was later alleged to have killed a bank manager outside London and imprisoned in Switzerland following the murder of a taxi driver, although he was sent back to England to finish the sentence. To say that he was a pretty menacing chap would be a gross understatement.

But the place was full of guys who were unpredictable, to say the least. Take Frankie Bond; at the age of seventeen he killed a man in Walton Prison over an argument about his week's wages, which was three old pennies. He escaped the gallows because the death penalty had been suspended for five years as a trial period. He worked right above me in the quarry. I was breaking rocks while he and another prisoner were drilling holes for the gelignite when I heard them arguing about a game of chess. The next thing I knew, there was a thud and a guy's body was lying beside me. Frank had hit him with a 14lb hammer. He looked down and said in a matter-of-fact way, 'You heard him keep arguing all of the time.' Frank was later to cut another prisoner's throat in the church for arguing with him (this guy was luckier – he survived).

There were hundreds of similar incidents, but one prisoner working in the mail-bag shop took the prize for holding a grudge the longest. He accused the inmate working in front of him of stealing one of his mail bags. The guy didn't like being accused and so he turned around and punched his accuser on the nose, was placed on report and got the usual three days' bread and water for assaulting another prisoner. He then returned and sat in his old place of work. Now in the workshop they used to stencil 'Post Office' on all of the mail bags and would collect a small drop of white spirit each day to dilute the stencil ink. The guy who had been punched collected a little drop each day and put it into a sauce bottle. When he had filled it up, he calmly poured it over the chap in front of him and set light to it.

Not everyone was homicidal. The nicest people I met in Dartmoor in those days were the old London Airport robbery gang, Jimmy and George Woods, Sammy Ross and others. They had attempted the biggest robbery of the time but got caught and were sentenced to twelve and fourteen years even though no one got hurt. They did their sentence and just smiled their way through it.

But the prison, with its violence and brutality, was beating so many people. The child molesters probably suffered more than anyone. In those days there was no Rule 43, whereby a prisoner can ask to be kept segregated from the rest of the prisoners. Even worse, every prisoner had a card which was placed outside the cell door on a wooden board. Roman Catholics would have a red card, Church of England a white card and Jews would have a blue card. In those days they were the only religions considered. If a chap came through the reception and was asked, 'What's your religion?' and replied 'Muslim', he'd get remarks like 'Oh! We've got a clever one here guv, give him a blue card so he can pray with his mates.' On each card was written what sentence you were doing and where you were sentenced; on the back of the card was written your offence. If you were a child molester the screws always turned the card around when you were allocated to your cell, to make sure that when the prisoners surfaced to slop out they would all see it. From that day on your life would be hell. Child molesters were considered the lowest form of human life and the screws encouraged the other cons to give them plenty of treatment.

In Dartmoor two cells on the ground floor of each wing were used as a library where you could change your books once a week. The average con would pick out three or four easy-to-read novels. But the child molesters used to pick the thickest books they could find and put them into their waistband to make it harder for chaps to stick knives in them as they were passing on the landing.

In those days there never seemed to be any shortage of places to put mentally disturbed people, so if a man or woman went to court for any type of offence and there was a doubt about his or her sanity, the judge would remand them for a psychiatric report. They would go to the hospital, within the prison, and after a couple of weeks go back to the courts to be sentenced. If they had to have treatment or to be kept away to protect society, then that would follow. There was no delay and it was also the case that people who had been driven to insanity whilst in prison could always be found a place. Nowadays, the government is spending millions of pounds on building new prisons, but they've closed lots of hospitals and psychiatric wards which has put some people, in my view, out into society who cannot cope. It appears to me that these people are ending up in prison, where they should not be, and may cause much of the violence and destruction within the prisons.

There was a doctor at Dartmoor, when I first went there, who seemed to have no trouble finding places for mentally-disturbed prisoners. There always seemed to be someone on the way to a secure mental home each week. Unfortunately it was this same doctor who caused so many people to break down. If you had some reason for seeing him you would report sick to your landing screw first thing in the morning. Then when everyone else went to work you would stay in your cell. The doctor would start his rounds in the company of one of the medical screws and an orderly who carried a bottle of liquid aspirin. These would be typical remarks between the prisoner and the doctor, and it would be funny if it wasn't so tragic.

'What's wrong with you?'

'I can't sleep, Doctor.'

'Right, get this man's mattress out of his cell if he can't sleep on it, and give him some medicine.'

Or, to a prisoner with alopecia, 'What's wrong with you?'

'My hair is falling out, Doctor.'

'Right, give him an envelope to keep his hair in and give him some medicine.'

If any prisoner mentioned anything wrong internally, he was immediately put on a water diet. This kind of treatment would invariably cause the prisoner to end up in the punishment block for shouting some abuse at the doctor. It was a vicious circle that caused men to break down completely.

One of the jobs I had in Dartmoor, after coming off the quarry, was No. 3 party, responsible for a variety of tasks inside the prison walls. It was made up of a motley crew of murderers, armed robbers and con-men. In fact in the year or so I was on it there was practically every type of crook and villain, from every part of the British Isles, working on that party. Charles Dickens would have painted a beautiful picture of the characters who came and went. We had the task of emptying the rubbish bins from the cell blocks, the kitchen, the hospital and offices. We were also responsible for conveying food from the victualling stores to the kitchen. Consequently we had plenty of chances to convey more than just legitimate goods. We were, in fact, the unofficial means of conveying all types of contraband from messages to betting slips plus the stakes, which were always tobacco, the universal currency of all prisoners. We worked on a commission from the prison bookmaker. We always knew of any impending transfers or in fact any other classified information concerning the prison, through our own 'artful dodger', namely Paddy Wormsley, who had the useful ability of reading a piece of paper upside-down.

Every Friday we would take the hard tack food from the stores to the kitchen where we would be given a can of tea, the real stuff not the gnat's pee that was usually served in the cell blocks. Friday was also the day when the kitchen staff made the jam tarts for the Sunday sweet. They were made in trays about two feet long and eighteen inches wide and then left to cool down before being dissected into about fifty portions and put into a shelved trolley until Sunday.

One Friday we decided to pinch one of the newly cooked jam tarts that lay cooling by the side of the ovens. Paddy elected to do the deed while we kept the kitchen screw otherwise occupied. He folded the large jam tart in half and put it down the front part of his overalls, buckled the bib back over and pulled his jacket around so that the tart was hidden from view. We then made our way hastily from the kitchen to the safety of our shed. But on the way Paddy began to look very uncomfortable and his face gradually contorted into an expression of extreme pain until he could no longer control himself and let out a yelp. The tart that he'd put down his overalls had only just come out of the oven and the jam was still baking hot and had started to run down his body. Paddy, who didn't wear underpants, was being burnt in some very tender places indeed. By the time we got to the safety of our shed, Paddy had sustained some pretty severe burns. It was clear that he would have to have some medical treatment, but it would be difficult to report sick. So we decided to pick the rubbish up from the hospital and see if we could get something from the orderly who was a rather effeminate character. He said he would get some stuff and even offered to apply it to Paddy's tender parts. Paddy quickly declined the offer and said he would put it on himself. We then went back to get rid of the evidence, which we did by eating the lot. Paddy was in pain for a few days but it wasn't long before he was back to his chirpy self again.

Some of the other characters on this particular party had made a name for themselves for one reason or another. One was Jimmy Essex, a tiny little chap who didn't weigh eight stone but was one of the most feared men in prison at this time. He had already killed two men and had attacked another, an ex-heavyweight boxer, whilst in Parkhurst

Prison. As a result he had been transferred to Dartmoor. Jimmy always seemed to be angry about something but I could never take him seriously. He was always muttering to himself, 'I'm going to do him one day,' whenever someone upset him. I would smile and sometimes start laughing. He would demand to know why I was laughing at him and I would try to explain that I was just tickled by the thought of a little guy like him beating up a giant. This must have played on his mind because he was to prove himself dramatically.

One day he was grumbling about the new screw that had been put on his landing, moaning, 'He keeps digging me out.' We had all seen the new screw in Jimmy's wing, who was well over six foot and proportionately built. I said jokingly, 'Are you going to set about him, Jim?' Sure enough, next morning Jimmy never turned up for work. He was in the punishment block for putting the screw in hospital – he nearly lost his sight. It was a long time before we saw Jim again.

Then there was Harry Rose, a great little character who had a wonderful sense of humour and was always telling us some story or other about his days in Liverpool. I asked him one day how he got his teeth knocked out and he told me the most amazing tale. He said that he was going through a particularly hard time and had no money when a mate of his told him they could get a bite to eat or a bowl of soup at a certain church mission. So Harry went along with his friend and got right to the front pew so that they would be first up for the grub. But Harry's mate had forgotten to warn him that they were expected to sing a few hymns and say a few prayers before they got their meal.

The service was going on and on and Harry's stomach was beginning to rumble so Harry piped up and said, 'Could we have some grub before we sing any more hymns?'

He was immediately told to 'shush' by the vicar, whereupon Harry said indignantly, 'This is a con' and demanded a bowl of soup. At this the vicar came down from the altar and nutted Harry in the mouth. Harry told us that he'd never been hit so hard in his life. We asked him what happened next, knowing that he was a fearless fighting man. But Harry said, 'What could I do? You can't chin a vicar, can you?' That summed Harry up for me. He was a great chap.

CHAPTER NINE

Will Crime Pay?

I finished that sentence at Dartmoor with more bitterness than when I started. By now twenty-six or twenty-seven, I decided that I was going to make plenty of money and have some good times. I'd met some pretty experienced law-breakers whilst I was in the 'Moor and I came out with the intention of putting a few things I'd learned into practice.

One of the first chaps I teamed up with was Bobby Connolly. He was just a little older than myself, and he had a good team around him. Bob was a pretty good 'peterman' (safe-cracker) and in those days the old Hobbs, Banhams and Chubbs were a push-over. It took a quarter of an hour to blow a safe and we had some pretty rich pickings. It wasn't long before I was banging a few peters myself.

Then I found a new life opening up in the nightclubs in London and Paris. It would cost about £20 for a return flight to Paris and I started to discover the delights of places like the Lido on the Champs-Elysées, the Moulin Rouge, the Lucky Stripe and some of the wonderful bars in the Place Pigalle in Montmartre. Whenever I came back to London I'd see old pals like Jack the Hat and tell him about the good time we were having in Paris but I could never talk him into coming. I don't think he fancied flying.

Of course, the good times cost money and as soon as the

coffers were empty we'd look around for a new safe to rob. Usually this took a certain amount of preparation but sometimes it all seemed so easy. I remember we were all at a party over Christmas, myself, Jack and Bob, and were having a nice drink when we were interrupted by a guy anxious to tell us about a peter in a place less than a mile away. At first we were not interested – we had no gelignite within miles of us and anyway we were enjoying ourselves. Eventually his enthusiasm and persistence began to get to us so we decided to go and have a look. As soon as we got to the place where the peter was supposed to be Jack and I went around the back to break in and in no time we were looking at an old Reliance 5-cwt 'box peter', one of the easiest to open. Jack and I decided we'd put it in the motor and take it back to the party, which was in a flat above a sweetshop in Stratford.

First, however, we had to negotiate the peter down a stairway. Jack got his hands under the bottom while I held the top. He had only taken a couple of the stairs, with me above him, when I felt the safe slipping from my grip. I yelled a warning and he flung himself aside just in time as the safe went hurtling down the stairs. He would have been dead had it hit him. Bob came running to tell us to keep the noise down but within two minutes the safe was in the motor and we were on our way back to the party. We put it in the cellar under the sweetshop and carried on having a drink.

The guy that told us about the safe couldn't keep still; he kept begging, 'There's thousands in it, can't we open it now?' We told him to be patient and wait until the morning. We all got our heads down for what was left of the night and went down to the cellar the next morning. The first thing we saw down there was the guy with the information sitting on the safe, too excited to sleep. But we realized why when we opened it. It was one of the biggest tickles we had ever had up to that time and it gave me the chance to relax and look up some of my old friends.

I had recently started to use the Barry club in Marylebone. The proprietor was an old friend from my school days, Dave Barry, and the clientele were a mixed bag of villains, con-men, solicitors, actors and a few of the well-known press people. One of the latter was Eddie Chapman who worked as a journalist for a Sunday paper called *Reynolds News*. Eddie Chapman had a fascinating and dangerous life and his story was portrayed in a film called *The Triple Cross*. He originated from the North-East and came to London as a youngster. He graduated from a petty thief to become an accomplished safe cracker, after doing a few stretches in prison, and even became very selective about the type of safes he was doing. He went over to Jersey on a job but was arrested and sentenced to three years' hard labour. This was just after the start of the Second World War and Eddie was stuck in prison when the Germans invaded the Channel Islands. Being clever, he devised a plan to get back home. In the course of talking to the German commandant, who had taken over the prison, he let it be known how much he hated the British government and admired the Third Reich. He impressed the Germans so much that he was interviewed by the Gestapo and taken back to Germany. He was asked to work as a saboteur for Germany and to let the Germans know of troop movements and the locations of any important targets. He was also encouraged to use his expertise as a peterman to gather potentially useful information. He agreed and was put through a training course, given equipment, explosives and a radio.

However the Germans, being careful, decided to test Eddie first and pretended to drop him over East Anglia. But instead they had gone to great lengths to set up an area in France with all the trappings of the English countryside. They dropped Eddie over this area and observed him. Luckily Eddie spotted something that caused him to guess that he was in German-occupied territory, so he carried on as he was supposed to. The Germans were now satisfied that they had a good man for the job and sent him out on a real mission – to sabotage the munitions factory at Enfield. He was dropped at night over Norfolk and immediately got in touch with the authorities. It took a little time to convince them that the story he was telling them was the truth as his record showed he was supposed to be in prison in Jersey. Once they were convinced, however, they asked him if he would be prepared to work for British Intelligence. He agreed but asked, 'What about the factory at Enfield?' He was told that an explosion would be arranged and an appropriate news bulletin would report that saboteurs were being blamed. Eddie successfully worked as a double agent until he was captured by the Russians near the end of the war and was interned in a Russian prison camp. He subsequently escaped and made it back to the British sector. He came back to England as a hero.

Eddie was a frequent visitor to the Barry club, as was a guy called Sir Sidney Cain. 'Sir Sid' was a con-man of some repute. He was a fascinating chap who had all the trappings of the landed gentry but was, in fact, the son of a Liverpool house painter. He spoke beautifully and looked the business in his cashmere and vicuña overcoats, a carnation ever present in his lapel.

Sidney used to entertain us with stories of his successful attempts to con some of the more gullible titled and wealthy people in the country. One of his favourites was the saga of how he nearly married the Wills Tobacco heiress. It was ony because he was exposed by the *Sunday People* that he failed to accomplish his plan. He told us about the time he took his 'man' to stay at the Wills' mansion for the weekend. His personal servant happened to be one of the best jewel thieves in London at that time. When Sir Sid went down for breakfast the next morning his prospective bride informed him that the butler had observed his man wandering around the house in the middle of the night checking all the windows and doors. Sir Sidney immediately told her that he was always the same, being extremely security conscious. Pretending to be embarrassed, Sir Sidney assured her he would have a word and tell his valet that security in the Wills' house was impregnable. When I knew Sir Sidney, he was married to an heiress from Alderney who was also a Marquesa.

Eddie Chapman was writing a book entitled *The Gentlemen of Crime* and Sir Sidney was featured in it, so we spent hours going around together while Eddie elicited stories from Sir Sidney. We must have seemed a strange combination, Eddie, David Barry, Sir Sidney and myself. It wasn't long before the Old Bill became intrigued enough to put a friendly 'eye' on our tail but as we were using some of London's more up-market watering-holes, the Old Bill stood out more than we did. They must have hated that particular job as Sir Sidney would immediately inform the licensee and clientele, 'These gentlemen from Scotland Yard are only here to protect everyone. I must apologize for their heavy boots on this nice carpet.' But he always sent a drink over to them, and it wasn't long before they realized there was nothing criminal in four odd fellows meeting each day.

I took my friends over to the East End one evening to meet a guy called Bulla Ward who I had become very friendly with. He was the proprietor of the Bentley club in Aldgate, in partnership with a guy called Roy Stafford who had been the borough surveyor. A more incongruous pair it would be hard to imagine. Bulla was a heavy-set tough-looking guy with a large razor scar running the length of his face, compliments of Ronnie Kray after an argument. 'Staffy' on the other hand was slightly built, quiet and sophisticated. But they seemed to hit it off very well together.

The Bentley club was in Artillery Row, right in the middle of the original 'Jack the Ripper' territory. When I first took my friends to the club I could see the looks of concern passing between them until we actually got inside. The Bentley had become one of the more popular of the clubs that had sprouted up in the East End in those days. The clientele was the usual mixture of celebrities, gangsters and sportsmen. I had started to use the club regularly and I'd found that Roy Stafford seemed to enjoy the company of the more ambitious criminals who frequented the place. In talking to him one evening I learned that he had more than just a passing interest in crime. He held a very definite view that the average criminal never set his sights high enough and that with more planning and common sense most of the criminals who used his club would be able to retire in a very short time. He suggested that they should put more effort into looking at the larger movements of money and valuables rather than into the ordinary targets of banks and post offices. But it still came as a surprise to me when, shortly afterwards, the KLM bullion robbery was pulled off with absolute precision and the minimum of force. The thieves got away with £750,000 in gold bars. I read shortly after this that Staffy had been arrested as the Mr Big behind the robbery when he stepped off a plane in Switzerland.

However I think the most unusual chap I met in the Bentley club was Sidney Proud. He was the boss of a travel agency and Bulla introduced me to him one evening. I failed to see why Bulla found him so fascinating as he looked so out of place in the club, with his foppish clothes and bow tie. He kept suggesting to Bulla, 'You must bring Eric up to the office to meet my friends.'

'What's his game? Is he the other way?' I asked Bulla suspiciously.

'No, he just likes having tough guys around him. You'll be surprised when we go to his office tomorrow,' he replied.

I couldn't wait and so we arranged to meet the next day. Bulla called for me about noon and we went to Piccadilly Circus where Sid Proud had the Spanish Travel Bureau. It was a very well-appointed block of offices and appeared to be doing plenty of business. To my surprise I was then introduced to two members of his staff. They were Max and Alex Mosley, the sons of the well-known fascist Oswald

Mosley. Alex was a giant of a young man, Max a little shorter than his brother. They were both very polite and seemed nice company. It was arranged that we should all go to Soho for a drink as there were plenty of afternoon members' clubs open throughout the day. Sid insisted that we should go to Aggie Hill's club. Now Aggie's was a notorious club because Aggie had been married to gangster Billy Hill. When we arrived it was packed with the usual motley crew of entertainers and criminals. But there was one guy sitting at the bar, next to Aggie, who was a well-known member of parliament. The minute he set eyes upon Sidney he became very abusive. I couldn't allow this to carry on as Sidney was in my company so I told the MP to button his lip. With that, a big hefty guy stood up from a seat at the bar and started to remonstrate with me. I flattened him, which had an immediate effect upon the honourable member and everything went quiet. Aggie ordered a taxi for the MP and we all settled down to a good drinking session. When the guy got off the floor he was told to leave. Sidney was overjoyed.

Later that evening we all retired to Sidney's house in Kensington. I couldn't believe my eyes when I saw photographs all over the lounge of Sidney with Adolf Hitler and other Nazi Party bigwigs. There were also pictures of Sidney with the sons and daughters of the Nazi 'firm', and also of Mussolini's kids. He certainly moved in some very strong company. A little later in the evening he invited me into his office, a room inside the house, and gave me £500.

'That's for knocking that guy out this afternoon. I think I could do with you about me if you want the job?' he said.

I decided I would have to give the offer some thought

for a while. It seemed an easy way of earning a few quid but it could get a little involved. I told Sidney I would give him my answer in a day or so. In the mean time the five of us went out quite a bit together. We would eat most evenings in Casa Pepi where Sidney seemed to be very well known. I began to notice that some very strange people had started to turn up in the places we were using. These strange comings and goings were explained when the *Sunday People* ran a story about the 'man who has a shrine to Hitler'. Sidney offered me a lot of money to do something about the guy who had written the article. I thought that was a good moment to bail out.

It was about this time that I first met the Kray twins socially. They had the snooker hall in Eric Street and the Double R club in Bow. I had already met their older brother Charlie, who used to take the twins to Bill Kline's gym when I was training down there. They were both very good amateur boxers and Charlie was showing them to a big promotor from Canada who was very impressed with them. I found them to be very likeable people and they had a good name with everyone who spoke of them. But it wasn't until I got seven years shortly after this that I got to know them a lot better. That's when Ronnie got three years for wounding and Reggie later got eighteen months for demanding money, which some believed was a questionable charge as the Old Bill had been taking a bit of notice of them. It was their way of testing the water.

In those days it would be usual for all of the guys to go to Freddie Mills' night spot in Charing Cross Road. Although it was supposed to be a Chinese restaurant it was more of a meeting place for practically anyone; ex-fighters, entertainers and gangsters. There would always be plenty of drink flowing, a small cabaret and a happy and relaxed atmosphere. Freddie had a partner who was Chinese and whose name was Eric, I seem to recall. Freddie's wife Chrissie, whose father Ted Broadrib had managed Freddie's illustrious boxing career, would sometimes be present. She had been married previously to a heavyweight from South Africa named Don McCorkindale so the conversation generally revolved around boxing.

Sadly all was not well with Freddie and he died a violent death. For many years people have conjectured about whether Freddie committed suicide or whether he was murdered. I would bet my life that Freddie killed himself. He was getting himself involved with a lot of people who were very different from the types he had grown up with and his character seemed to change just before he died. I also don't believe there was anyone who was capable of sitting Freddie in the back of a car, pointing a gun in his face and pulling the trigger. As for the later theory that the Kray twins had anything to do with Freddie's death, it is totally ridiculous. Anyone who knew the twins would know that they both admired people like Freddie and if they had known that he was in financial difficulty they would have helped him out. The twins always had a great admiration for any guy who had made his living in the ring as they knew themselves what a hard business it was.

A case in point is the way they treated Ted Kid Lewis, the ex-welterweight champion of the world, arguably the best fighter this country has ever produced. Kid Lewis had had an illustrious career in America where he fought Jack Britton, one of the all-time great fighters, and beat him to gain the world title. He was to have twenty epic battles with Britton over the years which caught the imagination of every fight fan on both sides of the Atlantic, none more so than Sophie Tucker, the last of the Red-Hot Mommas. She had a soft spot for The Kid. I remember being at Vallance Road one morning when Reggie told me that The Kid was coming to the house that day. They were going to fit him up with a suit and other smart gear as they were taking him to see Sophie Tucker at the Talk of the Town. They also arranged for a big bouquet to be sent backstage with a card saying 'To Sophie from Ted'. When Sophie came on stage they all had tears in their eyes as Sophie talked to Ted from the stage, reminiscing about the days in the twenties when Sophie Tucker was one of the biggest stars in America and Ted was the world champion.

As well as safe-cracking I was also having a few unlicensed boxing matches. Butty Sugrue had set up a ring in the Carlton club and was making more money with a few ex-pros and street fighters than the average boxing promoter. He was an incredible guy who came over from Ireland with a team of strongmen. They used to go around the pubs challenging all comers to various feats of strength that normally featured a barrel of beer. Butty could lift a man with his teeth, while the guy was sitting on a chair. For some pretty substantial bets he would bury himself in a coffin for twenty-four hours. There was obviously some trick to it but everyone was very impressed. He had a sidekick called Bert Azorati who was the ex-world wrestling champion. Bert was one of the toughest men I ever met and when things got a little rough, which they usually did when the Irish boys thought they had been duped over some of the results in the boxing ring, Bert would be there to sort it out. Bert seemed to positively enjoy people picking chairs up to use as a weapon against him. He wouldn't duck or ward off the blow, he'd just 'nut' the chair and stand with a big grin while his antagonist would make a quick exit.

I got involved with Butty and his team as a boxer in his 'gee' fights, from which we were all getting a few quid. A 'gee' fight is one that has been rehearsed before the customers arrive and only we know the result, so all of the betting done was pretty much in our favour.

I also became friendly with Jack Rosa, a professional thief who had gained notoriety through his battles with the authorities in prison. After many years of the same type of treatment that I had received Jack had attacked a screw pretty badly and had been sent to the Old Bailey for trial. With only about three weeks of his existing sentence to go, he was sentenced to a further five years. We had a lot in common and used to swap stories about the brutality we had both experienced – Jack, like myself, had also been flogged with the cat-o'-nine-tails. When I first met him he looked as if he had been through some tough times but the first thing one noticed about Jack was his quiet demeanour. He seemed a gentle guy but very determined. Although Jack was from South London we did our socializing mainly in the West End or the East End.

One place I was spending a fair amount of time in was a 'speiler' gambling club in Clarendon Road, Notting Hill Gate. These old-type speilers had an atmosphere all of their own. Whilst supposedly legitimate they had the feel of illegal gambling joints. There was none of the respectful air and subtle chink of chips that you found in a casino. It was ready cash only in a speiler and no one took their coats off. A few bums, often ex-thieves, would stand around ready to run errands, hoping to cop a few quid if a friend won. The clubs would attract the aristocracy and others from affluent backgrounds who would rub shoulders with the flamboyant fast living criminal fraternity. It would be quite usual to see Lord and Lady Docker gambling with Peter Scott, rated as Britain's most successful cat burglar, who lost fortunes in the speilers. When £300,000 worth of jewellery was stolen from Sophia Loren whilst she was filming at Elstree, Peter was suspected of the crime. Although there was never any proof, his status grew as a result of the allegation.

One would always know that a big game was in progress when Peter's 'Roller' was parked outside the speiler. I often saw 'Taffy' Raymond and 'Taters' Chapman leaving the club after losing quite heavily, return within the hour and sit down with the governor of the place, haggle over a piece of jewellery they had just acquired and then go straight back into the game. Occasionally poker games would go on for days with some guys just taking a short nap before going back to the table. However there was never any trouble and there was always good-humoured banter between the punters who arrived at regular intervals. Some of the greatest characters, from all walks of life, would use the various speilers which were dotted all over London.

Occasionally one place would become more popular than the others and Clarendon Road was one of the favourites at this time. 'Shaky Sheila', a lady who ran a number of 'clip joints' in Soho, was a frequent visitor to the speiler. A clip joint was a near-beer place with a number of sexy girls encouraging mainly tourist punters to buy the exotic-looking drinks at exhorbitant prices and promising to meet them when they finished 'work'. But the girls never turned up at the meeting place and if the punter returned to complain he would be fobbed off by a menacing bouncer. Sheila was from Liverpool and was a great favourite in the speiler. She would earn fortunes in the clip joints but would lose nearly every penny at the dice table.

Clarendon Road was where I renewed my acquaintance with my old colleague Joey Mayo, from St Vincent's Approved School. Joe had grown into a handsome guy over six feet tall with curly fair hair who always had an attractive girl with him. One night Joe told me about two girls who were using a flat directly opposite the speiler to 'entertain' their clients. One of their clients was a well-known MP whose special fetish was that he liked to be treated as a skivvy. Joe arranged for myself and a couple of mates from the old Nash gang to go up on to the veranda where we could get a good view through the french windows into the flat. We couldn't believe our eyes when we saw who the client was. He was well known by sight to us all. When the girls started to verbally abuse him and threaten him with a beating we could hardly contain ourselves as he cringed and pleaded with his 'tormentors'. The spectacle continued but when the girls took his trousers down and started to beat his bottom we could not stop ourselves from bursting out laughing. When he heard this he came to the french windows and stood there fuming whilst we pointed to his diminishing manhood. We then went back to the speiler and left the girls to convince him that they didn't know who we were. They must have done a good job as I often saw his car parked outside the flat after this incident. I sometimes wondered how he must have felt when a question was asked in the House about the growing industry in pornography and the dangers involved to the fabric of society. Well, the industry has certainly prospered since those days and I know many people, supposedly pillars of society, who have indulged and also many who have become wealthy as a result.

But who were we to moralize, we were just a bunch of crooks who spent hours in the gambling dens. Anyway I had other things to think about. I had pulled off a couple of raids that had netted me a fair junk of money and I knew the police were making their presence felt around the circles I was moving in. I knew I had to be careful and try to keep a low profile but it is very hard to be involved in major crime and at the same time stay incognito.

CHAPTER TEN

Escape and the Cockney Millionaire

I was eventually arrested for a series of robberies that totalled many thousands of pounds. The police raided a flat in Bayswater to arrest myself and two of my pals but I managed to escape through a back window. However, I was caught in a gambling club in Notting Hill Gate later that night while arranging to get a false identity and was remanded in custody to Brixton Prison. After a series of identity parades at Brixton I was committed for trial at the Old Bailey. I knew I had a few months to wait for the trial and I was expecting to get a big sentence. Since I had by this time become pretty well known in London's underworld I thought I would have a fair chance of getting a bit of help to escape.

Then what seemed to be a bit of luck came my way. A couple of chaps I knew slightly were arrested for robbing a bank in Mitcham and I knew they would be interested in any plan that would afford a means of escape. But as soon as I approached them I was delighted to find they had already started to put their plans into operation. One of the guys, Teddy Rees, told me how they had been arrested and I thought they must already have had all the bad luck that they could have in a lifetime – which I hoped meant we should have some good luck in making good our escape.

Ted and his three pals had decided to rob a bank in Mitcham over a bank holiday weekend so that they would have until Tuesday morning to work without being disturbed. At first everything went according to plan. They gained access to the bank and fixed the alarms without any problems and whilst two of them were setting up the vault for blowing, the other two opened the big safe in the bank proper. The safe yielded £48,000 but the vault had jammed and they needed more 'jelly' to get into it. So it was decided that two of the gang would take the £48,000 home and pick up some more explosives whilst the other two would wait for them to return. Ted was one of the two who stayed in the bank. They expected to wait at the most about three hours; after twelve hours had elapsed they started to get a bit jittery. They were imagining all kinds of disasters, especially when they decided to phone one of the other guy's homes and found that he hadn't been back. Eventually they had to leave the bank. On the way out, while climbing over the wall, Ted gashed his finger on a piece of glass on top which cut out a lump of his glove at the same time. When they eventually arrived home they found that their companions had been stopped by an ordinary police check and were taken into the nick. The Old Bill couldn't believe the amount of money in their possession. They obviously wouldn't enlighten the law as to how they had acquired it and so were charged with possession on Tuesday and taken to the magistrates.

Later that day, when the word went out from the bank,

the Old Bill knew where the money had come from. When they went to the bank and found bloodstains around the walls they knew someone else was involved. But the unluckiest thing of all, from Ted's point of view, was that an eagle-eyed copper found a piece of Ted's glove and there inside the glove was preserved a nice piece of skin from Ted's finger. After the fingerprint people had done their work Ted was hauled in to explain how the piece of skin missing from his finger had ended up on a bank wall in Mitcham.

So here we all were, walking around the exercise yard plotting our escape, and the good thing was that Ted's other mate was still at large. We were all on the same landing and as luck would have it, I was in the cell opposite Ted's, which looked out on to a compound at the rear of the prison. It was decided that we would cut the bars in Ted's cell and if we could have the job completed by one of the coming Sunday mornings, Ted's friend would come over the wall of the compound and, when we dropped a cigarette packet as a signal, would throw a rope up to the cell.

Our first problem was getting the hacksaws into the prison, as people like us were pretty closely observed. Then we had another bit of luck. A guy called George Dawson came to Brixton on remand for allegedly ripping off the government over a consignment of orange juice. Dubbed the 'Cockney Millionaire', he had made a fortune out of scrap metal after the Second World War. He had a yacht in the South of France and would entertain government officials and the aristocracy at his home or in the Mediterranean. Therefore when he was arrested and sent to Brixton he was treated with respect. When we went to and from our court appearances we would be taken in the 'meat wagon', a large van with tiny cubicles down each side, with a very narrow piece of wood to sit on. We would each be locked into a cubicle and then, when we got to the prison, thoroughly searched. But George used to travel to and from court in a private car and would go straight back to his cell with just a perfunctory rub down. We set to work on him until, after a little cajoling, he agreed to bring the blades in for us.

The blades which Ted's friend brought to the court were only six inches long, of high-tension steel. He wrapped them in a rubber covering and put them in a greased condom and told George the best place to hide them. George was by this time becoming very reluctant to carry out the mission, and as he was about twenty stones in weight he had a bit of manipulating to do before he got the blades into place. Then, to everyone's horror, the screws who came to our cell to load us all up in the meat wagon said, 'You as well, Dawson, your car's not here today.'

George nearly died. We could hear him pleading with the screws, saying, 'There's no way I can get into a little space like that.' But the screws were adamant and eventually managed to squeeze him in to a cubicle. We were kept on the verge of hysterics all the way back to Brixton. Every time we went over a bump in the road we would hear George moaning piteously. But we did eventually get the blades back into the wing.

Now we had to set about a plan to cut the bars with the least amount of risk. It was decided that I would take my spy-hole cover off so that I could see as far as two or three cells on either side of Ted's cell. We then set about loosening the rail which ran the length of the landing. Anyone walking along the landing would make the rail shake and should we have any intrusion I would drop my chamber pot lid on the floor a couple of times to warn Ted.

This was going along OK until the con in the cell beneath me began shouting up complaints about my constantly dropping the lid of the pot. This started a bit of controversy, so after he'd left his cell the next morning to slop out I went and hit his light fitting with my shoe, hoping he would be moved to another cell. But no, they sent for the electrician and got him a new light fitting. Plan B was that I should knock him out and have him taken to hospital and this was soon accomplished with the desired effect.

Now we found another problem. We had started to fill the saw cut with nougat brought in on our visits and this had started to attract hundreds of flies. Everyone on the landing was complaining about this unusual plague and Ted's cell seemed to be full of them. It was amazing that the screws didn't get wind of what was happening. But at last it was the Saturday before the morning of the escape and Ted was certain that only the paint was holding the bars together.

We were going to have to move quickly on Sunday morning so we kept pressing Ted to make sure that the bars only needed a couple of rubs before they came apart. Ted decided just to give them a little touch-up prior to us going out to exercise, with the result that when he shut his door one of the bars fell down and hung loose. We were all very quiet in the yard and carefully watched every screw just to see if anybody had noticed anything amiss. The suspense was agonizing but we got back to the cells without incident and everything seemed normal. We were quickly trying to wedge in some matchsticks or anything we could find to hold the bar in place, thinking that everything was ready to go and we'd get away with it, when I heard the rail rattling slightly. I got up to look out of the spy-hole and there were about six screws creeping towards Ted's cell. I leapt over to the pot and banged it on the floor but my door was flung open at the same time as Ted's and we were taken down to the punishment cells. We were a little worried about Ted's mate coming the next morning but though he had actually got into the compound with the equipment, when the cigarette packet hadn't come over the wall as a signal to throw the rope, he aborted and left unseen.

CHAPTER ELEVEN

Is There a Mr Big?

After a trial at the Old Bailey I was sentenced to seven years and my friends both got five. On the same day one of my old pals, Jack Rosa, was given four years for another robbery. The screws at Wandsworth were far from happy to see the pair of us as they knew that Jack and I would not be standing for any of their bullying tactics. We were both put on the same landing in A Wing and it was funny the next morning, when the landing screw came to look in on the new faces, to hear him moaning that it wasn't fair: 'I've got the pair of them, I'm seeing the Chief about this.' He must have convinced the Chief as Jack was taken to another wing that afternoon.

In Wandsworth at that time there were many prisoners who were later to become quite notorious underworld figures. It is a common misbelief that behind every big crime committed there is a shadowy 'Mr Big' doing the planning and that the actual perpetrators of the crime are paid a set fee. Nothing could be further from the truth. In actual fact, most big crimes that have occurred in this country over the last thirty years have been planned and executed by people who I have known, either as friends or acquaintances. Most are ordinary criminals who have progressed up the ladder from petty thieves to being involved in the planning and execution of some of the world's biggest robberies. For instance the Great Train Robbery was planned and executed by quite a few of the chaps who I'd met through various stages of my life. I first met Douglas Goody whilst we were both on remand for ordinary crimes in our teens. He was a smash and grab specialist, who was incidentally sentenced to be birched for doing no more than the ram-raiders are doing today. Jimmy Hussey, like most criminals, came from a working-class background and as he got older he looked around, found that the more privileged in society were having a ball and decided that he'd also like to go dancing now and again. He got involved with a 'jump-up' firm, doing exactly the same type of thing that I was doing myself at that time – taking loads from lorries. We used to see each other quite often in Manchester in the fifties where, after a 'tickle', we'd end up at the same bars and parties. A good time was had by all, until Jimmy got five years for taking a lorry-load of cigarettes.

I met Ronnie Biggs and Bruce Reynolds in Wandsworth Prison in the fifties. We were all working in the brush shop. The no talking rule was in existence in those days, so you only got to know each other through brief snatches of conversation on the landings, on the way to and from work or the exercise yard. There would invariably be some poor chap on report every day, sentenced to three days' bread and water, seven days' solitary confinement and seven days' loss of remission for breaking the rule. So if you needed to convey any information to each other, it would be done by writing a 'stiff' on prison toilet paper.

Ronnie Biggs at that time was just a run of the mill professional thief. He pitted his wits against the law and when he was caught he expected to get a prison sentence and just as naturally he would try to escape. He was always a 'special watch' prisoner. Ronnie was tall and gangling with a permanent smile on his face. He had a friend called Terry who was very similar to Biggsy and the pair of them were always plotting their escape. They would frequently be given a 'dry bath', i.e. a strip search, but they usually managed to be one step ahead of the screws.

Ronnie Biggs also struck up a friendship with Bruce Reynolds which developed through their liking for jazz. In those days the only reading matter you were allowed to have sent in was either two magazines which were approved by the authorities, usually *Picture Post* and *Illustrated*, or your local paper, which would be heavily censored, and a trade magazine. The jails must have been full of musicians because the most popular paper in prison was the *Melody Maker*. Bruce Reynolds used to get it sent to him every week and he would lend it to Biggsy who once got a dose of bread and water for being in possession of another prisoner's magazine.

Bruce Reynolds was a serious thinker, even at that early age. He was in his twenties and he was doing four years for robbing a bookmaker. I've never seen a guy go to the lengths that he did to get time off his sentence. In fact he nearly lost his life over it.

It happened just after Ronnie Kray arrived at Wandsworth. Ronnie had been doing a three-year sentence for wounding a guy. He'd been sent to Grove Park Mental Hospital where the inmates were allowed to wear their own clothes. Reggie went to visit him there, wearing identical clothes to his twin brother, and just swapped places with him. When the 'nurses' came to tell Ronnie to go back to his cell, Reggie said, 'No, I'm Reggie. My brother's gone to arrange some tea for me.'

Of course, they realized they'd been duped, but they had to let Reggie go on his way and put a warrant out for Ronnie's arrest. After Ronnie was eventually caught, he was sent to Wandsworth and ended up in the brush shop, where we were all working. Bruce Reynolds came to me in the exercise yard and said, 'Do you think Ronnie would mind if I had a gun brought into the prison and put near where he is working?'

Ronnie couldn't have cared less because he knew he was going to do nearly all of the three-year sentence for his escape from Grove Park. Bruce arranged for a gun to be brought in by some friends and then went to the Governor to say that he'd heard there was to be a breakout and a gun had been hidden in the brush shop. Once the gun had been found, Bruce was told that he would be given a few months' remission off his sentence.

But this wasn't enough for Bruce who soon had another idea. He got someone to write a note threatening him for spoiling the escape plan and saying that he would be 'done'. He showed the note to the Chief Officer who immediately took him to the Governor. They both assured him that it was impossible for anyone to know it was him, as they were the only two people who had this information.

Nothing daunted, Bruce tried again. His next plan was for Frank Mitchell, 'The Mad Axeman', who had come back to Wandsworth after his second escape, to attack him in the bath-house. Frank was told there would be a few quid sent to his sister if everything was done according to plan and Bruce was to receive a superficial wound. Unfortunately no one planned for Frank's enormous strength. He nearly killed Bruce who was found weltering in his own blood in a bath cubicle. When I later asked Frank what went wrong, he said, 'I only meant to give him a little nick, but it went right through him.' Bruce Reynolds got a bit more time knocked off, but he also nearly got himself 'knocked off'.

Ronnie and Reggie were already well known in the London underworld as two pretty formidable characters – although they had not yet gained the national notoriety of later years. The story of the way they duped the staff at Grove Park earned them a different sort of respect from the cons in Wandsworth. Ronnie was very quiet and did not mix much with the other prisoners but by now I had gained something of a reputation so the twins were both very friendly and showed me respect. About a month after Ronnie was discharged Reggie Kray arrived doing eighteen months for demanding money. He and I hit it off right away and became as friendly as two people could do. We had a mutual respect for each other. Reggie would never let anyone push him around, although he kept a lower profile and probably stood for more pettiness than he would ordinarily as he was only doing eighteen months and was awaiting an appeal so he couldn't risk having too many fall-outs.

I was working in the main mail-bag shop at the time. George Dawson was sitting next to me and was still a bundle of nerves following his little escapade with the hacksaw blades. Reggie came in and sat in the same shop. As we were all on the back row, as far away from the screws as possible, we could have a chat without too much aggravation. One of the cons decided to relieve the boredom of the shop by sneaking up to the pile of finished mail-bags and setting fire to them. As the flames started to get bigger, the only one who couldn't see them was the screw in the observation box until George Dawson helpfully shouted, 'Fire, sir!' He didn't realize that he risked getting set upon by half the cons in the workshop, he was just reacting naturally. So Reggie and I had a few words with the chaps and it was all forgotten.

Just after this incident, Reggie and I were on a visit together. Ronnie came up to see Reggie and Charlie came up to see me. As Ronnie got up to leave he noticed a guy on our side of the visiting room who had upset him before he went out. Ronnie started to give him a coating and just as the bloke went to open his mouth to verbal Ronnie back, Reggie flattened him and had to do a bit of 'bread and water'.

Shortly after this, Reggie was discharged following a successful appeal. On the day he was released he gave all the possessions that he'd accumulated in prison to me and promised to keep in touch. He said, 'By the time you get out we should be doing well in business and you won't want for anything.' Most people in prison make such promises to their friends, promises to keep in touch, to do some little thing for the family, and promptly forget them when they get out. Not so the twins – they spent a lot of time thinking of the people they had left inside, remembering little things like sending a book or ensuring that some kid had a Christmas present sent to him 'from his dad who was away at work'. Most cons respected the twins for this side of their characters. I had this feeling for Reggie especially as he was the one who always kept in touch to see if I needed anything. In fact the twins had their own particular friends and it was noticeable that certain members of the 'Firm' would be closer to one or other of them – though in all it was one big happy family.

Wandsworth was always known to be a very violent prison but there would sometimes be considerable humour about the place. Quite a lot of light relief which existed in many of the prisons in those days focused around the homosexual prisoners who had been sentenced to fairly long terms. Some were quite tragic figures but, in general, most were amusing and had a good sense of humour. Nearly all had female names and they would stand out immediately due to their plucked eyebrows, the rouge made from the dye of book covers and their pronounced mincing walks. Some came from good families whilst others were basically runaways who had been persecuted. But whatever their particular background they would all be treated as weirdos by the courts – which is the last thing that they were. In fact most were very intelligent and well able to look after themselves in any verbal contest. It was very noticeable that most of the screws made sure that they never became involved in arguments with the gays as they were normally made to look pretty foolish.

I remember two well from my time in Wandsworth. Pat and Paula were both very different, Pat being tall and self-confident whilst Paula was very petite and very nervous when he first arrived in the nick. However, Pat soon took Paula under his wing and in no time at all Paula was mincing around with all of the assurance of an old timer.

It was quite common knowledge that some other prisoners would become very friendly with the gays and the odd screw would also show favours to them. In the evenings, when certain screws were on duty, one would hear the sound of a spring lock slotting into place as they crept around the landings, paying visits to the 'girls'. We would question the individual who we knew had received a visitor the previous evening. If it was someone like Pat he would be very open and say, 'Oh him, he comes to see me once a week. I have to talk dirty to him and give him "one off the wrist", but it makes my life a lot easier in here.'

But it wasn't all so humorous. There was once a very violent knife fight in D Wing involving a gay, called Bobby, who had been seeing two different blokes at the same time. Both of these guys had reputations as hard men and it eventually erupted into a bloody battle as one of them, who was besotted with Bobby, decided to take the life of his rival. But the potential victim managed to wrestle the knife away from his assailant and in turn inflicted some horrendous wounds on him. Strangely enough this incident wasn't considered any more serious than any of the other acts of violence which occurred regularly in that establishment. In fact it was treated with humour by most of the inmates with comments like, 'I hear there has been a bit of domestic trouble in the married quarters.'

It wasn't long after this incident that I heard that I was on the transfer list. My allocation had come through and I was sent back to Dartmoor.

CHAPTER TWELVE

Back to the 'Moor

Having been in Dartmoor once before. I knew exactly what was waiting for me. First there was the cold and dank surroundings. Moss covered the cell walls; photographs on your shelf would curl up with the moisture. Your bed was always damp. This was in the ordinary wings. The punishment block was unbelievable – even colder and wetter; absolutely silent except for the occasional cries and shouts of the people being beaten. I spent a few years in that punishment block without seeing another prisoner, just hearing their screams of anger or pain. And any prisoner might find himself in the punishment block, accused of offences against the good order and discipline of the prison.

This typical scenario will illustrate how easy it was to get put into the punishment block. I spent thirteen and a half years in Dartmoor Prison and a few of those years were spent in the prison quarry. Our job was to break the rocks with a 14lb hammer until they were small enough to go into the crusher which would reduce them to stones for road making and breeze blocks. This was a very arduous task – you were not allowed a break except for the lunch period. You were not allowed to speak. There were screws observing you all the time, either from the floor of the quarry or from the gun turrets, one near the entrance to the quarry and one in a type of sentry post above us. When we were marched back into the prison we passed the 'tally point' where the Chief and his sidekick would stand taking the numbers. For instance, if there were sixty-five men working on the quarry, the screw in charge of discipline would come by and usually say, 'Sixty-five, all correct and two reports.' This would mean that there were two prisoners on report in the morning for some breach of discipline. That was a guaranteed loss of remission, bread and water diet and a minimum of a week in the punishment block. On the rare occasions when the screws would come by and say, 'Sixty-five, all correct and no reports,' the Chief would narrow his eyes and look very pained. If this was repeated over a period of a few days, the Chief would call the discipline screw back and say, 'Do you mean to tell me that you've got sixty-five convicts working in the quarry and not one of them has broken a prison rule in the last three days? I don't think you can be doing your job properly. I'll have to make a note of that.'

Everyone on the quarry would be aware that someone would have to go on report the next day, so they all made sure that they just kept on belting those rocks without any let up. Late in the day, when it was obvious that no one was going to do anything wrong, some poor sod would notice the screw standing next to him.

'You know you're not supposed to talk whilst working.'

'I ain't talking, Guv.'

'Are you calling me a liar, prisoner? Take that threatening look off your face.'

The con would try talking his way out of trouble, but he would find himself on report with five or six charges, typically that he was lazy, persistently talking and when told about it adopted a threatening attitude and used abusive and foul language. This would usually earn the poor chap fourteen days' loss of remission, three days' No. 1 diet and seven days' No. 2 diet plus fourteen days confined to cell, in addition to receiving plenty of abuse.

Unfortunately this was just the usual run of the mill stuff that the average prisoner put up with and no one took any real notice of it. However, there were a few cons in the 'Moor who were prepared to stand up and be counted and not just take the knocks. This helped a lot of the other cons to get on with their time.

I was only in the prison a matter of days before I was put in the punishment block. My file made it clear to the authorities that I was one of the handful of prisoners who wouldn't stand their sadistic ways. I think that the majority of prison staff just wanted to get their job done, draw their wages at the end of the week and go home to their families. But there were always a crowd who took pleasure in inflicting as much misery as they could – with the result that all the screws became hated. A con who had been involved in an incident and been subjected to some degree of violence in the punishment cells would probably feel that he wanted revenge. Then something harmless would set him off – for instance a screw might unintentionally walk into him. Even though this screw was not involved in the violence he'd suffered, the con would lash out, seeing only the uniform. No one would think of looking to the cause of what they would term an unprovoked attack on a member of staff. Instead the heavy mob would arrive to administer the expected beating and the cycle would start again.

It would take a prisoner about three months to finish his punishment after an attack on a member of staff. This would include a period on bread and water and then a period of CC. On one occasion I was given three lots of this punishment, plus the beatings, all to run consecutively and several times I was sentenced to Rule 36, 'that the prisoner will be kept segregated from the rest of the prisoners for the good order and running of the prison'. In this case I would have no idea when I would be released.

The most upsetting feature about these long periods in the punishment block was the silence broken only by the distant sounds of violence or the odd shout of 'Bastards!' by some con who managed to remain defiant. Worst of all was the sobbing of some prisoners who were completely beaten and despairing.

To be fair the odd member of staff would show some pity or humanity. Sometimes when you collected your bedclothes from outside the cell at night you would find a book hidden inside the roll. And the chaplain might call to see you and perhaps bring a book. But these little gestures of kindness were few and far between.

There were a few cons in those days who I will always remember and admire for their guts, as I spent many years in the punishment block with them. Tommy Flanagan was one in particular. His determination and courage could only be measured by the men who knew the odds that he fought against. Tommy spent many years in Dartmoor's punishment block, but they never looked like breaking him. Instead he broke a few of them.

During my second term there Dartmoor was going through an exceptionally violent period. One con had been found dead in B Wing in funny circumstances and it had been hushed up as another suicide. I was actually in the hospital wing, in a strongbox called the strip cell, when I heard screams of terror from a guy called Nelson in the padded cell next to me. I could hear the thudding of the sticks on his head and body and his voice pleading with them to stop. It wasn't until later that I learned he died after this beating that occurred that day and night. I was later to read in the local press that the Coroner had asked how he got so many appalling injuries and the prison doctor said he had thrown himself against the walls of his cell. Considering he was in a padded cell at the time and that it was standard practice to use a strait-jacket on prisoners in these circumstances, which they may well have done, I find it hard to believe that even they could have got away with that one.

I've recently been back to Dartmoor to photograph the place where Nelson was buried with a little stone showing his initials and the year. I would bet that the validity of everything I say about the prison authorities could be proved by the exhumation of his grave.

As the years passed, some members of the heavy mob stood out as being unusually sadistic, even by their standards, with a fascination for beating men between the legs and trying to put their batons into some pretty painful places. One bloke liked to boast that he was a boxer of some repute. He was always sparring up to people, and even if most people there would have liked to have taken up the challenge they knew the consequences so they just put up with his bullying. But a few of us knew that he was

I recently revisited the site of St Vincent's Approved School.
It seems symbolic that only the old whipping post remains
standing.

My mother did not have an easy life with four boys to bring up. She is shown here with my brothers Brian (*left*) and Fred (*right*).

My father was a well-respected local character. Here he is standing on the left of the football team he managed in his spare time. My brother Fred is in the middle row, second from the left.

Dartmoor Prison, where I spent a total of thirteen years, most of them in this wing.

The entrance to the quarry at Dartmoor, the scene of much violence as well as several escapes.

I used to see the Krays sometimes in Freddie Mills' restaurant so Teddy Smith, who I had introduced to Reg, sent me a copy of this picture whilst I was in prison. From the left are: Teddy Smith, Mickey Forsyth, Johnny Davis, Reg, Freddie Mills, Ron, Dickie Morgan and Sammy Leaderman.

The twins always kept in touch with the world of boxing. They are seen here sitting next to the great Sonny Liston whose UK tour they were involved in.

I went with the twins on a trip to Newcastle where we visited La Dolce Vita club. Sitting round the table are, from the left, Mickey Forsyth, Billy Daniels, Reg, Johnny Squibb, a friend of Billy's, Johnny Davis, a guy called Peter, myself and Ron.

Curly King (*right*) is an old friend of mine from our days in Soho who also took up with the twins. He is pictured here with Reg.

Dudley Grace (*centre*) and I had many great times together in our gambling days. Johnny Quirk on the right is a great mate from Bristol.

Jimmy the Weed (*left*) with Dave Moore and Ronnie Knight (*right*). Jimmy may be small but he has the heart of a lion.

Jimmy and I have enjoyed some great evenings together with actor Mark McMannus, who is pictured here between myself and the Weed. His wife Marion is standing behind him while my wife Carole is behind Jimmy on the right.

Lennie Peters was a good friend who always kept in touch. Carole and I would take him out for a drink to our local whenever he was in the area.

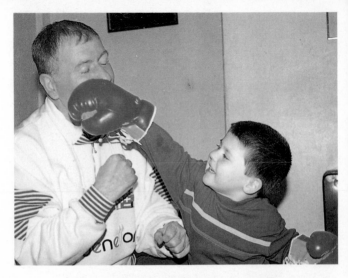

My son Michael is a chip off the old block.

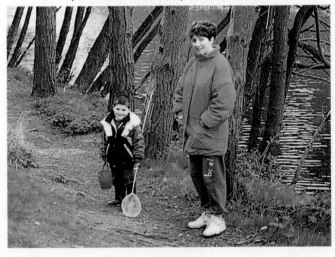

Carole and Michael on a walk by the River Nidd, close to our house in Harrogate. It's a far cry from the days when my only view was a prison wall.

always diving down to the punishment block whenever the 'fun' was going on. It was decided therefore that he should be 'done' himself. There were probably half a dozen guys in our wing who could have taken care of him. But it was felt that he had to be given a hiding in front of everyone, by one prisoner, to show him for what he really was – a coward and sadist. I said I wanted to be the one to perform this task, so it was agreed that we'd wait until he was on duty in the evening. I wanted as many men as possible to see what he was really made of. I sat around with Tommy Flanagan, Cyril, Don Adams and Lennie Crooks, waiting for the one and a half hour session, when we were allowed to associate with each other, to come to an end. I said to them, 'Don't get involved and leave it to me, it's got to be a man-to-man thing to prove the point.'

Finally the screw shouted, 'Right, pack up, back to your cells.'

I stood up and said, 'It's too early, we've another five minutes yet.'

He replied, 'You heard what I said, get back to your cells right now.'

I then asked him if he thought he could put me in my cell. I could tell by his face that he realized this was a confrontation. He was looking around for help and all he could see was the pitiless faces of cons looking at him. I said quietly, 'Don't worry, it's just you and me. No one else is getting involved. I'm going to show everyone what a coward you are.'

He started saying, 'Look, just go back to your cell and I'll forget what you said. You'll hear no more about it.'

I knew his bottle had gone, so I said, 'If you can really fight on your own, start fighting because that's the only way out for you. It's just you and me.'

With that I hooked him to the belly. He had no chance. All the frustration and pent-up anger rose up in me. I wouldn't let him drop. I just kept smashing him in the doorway of one of the cells until finally I stood back and let him slump to the floor.

By this time, about six or seven screws had arrived with the Chief. I just stood looking at them and my pals walked towards them. Tommy Flanagan acted as spokesman. He said to the Chief, 'If he gets done in the chokey block, I am going to hold you personally responsible.'

I can only say that Tom's words must have had some effect for as I walked to the punishment block it was the first and only time that I never got a beating. In fact the Chief brought Tom down to the strongbox to make sure that the heavy mob hadn't given me the usual treatment. It started to dawn on me then that maybe I was winning my battle with the authorities.

It was after my punishment for this assault on a screw had finished that I met Obedyne face to face. I first heard of him in the mid-fifties: a Nigerian of abnormal strength, he was one of the most fearful characters that they ever had to deal with in the prison system. They used to say he was mad, but I got to know him pretty well and didn't find him so. I think it was a case of the system creating its own monster and then not knowing how to control it. It is my view from my experience that some of the police and the prison staff were racist. It was bad enough if you dared to object to their treatment of you, but if you were black as well then God help you. There were not many black guys in prison in those days, so consequently there were one or two who were sent to jail who I encountered who had a pretty bad time. This was the case with Obedyne.

He had originally been arrested for not having a ticket when he came through Notting Hill Gate Tube station. There was an incident in which the ticket collector received a punch. Obedyne then ran off. The police were called and someone who knew Obedyne told them where he lived. The police duly arrived at Obedyne's flat, where they immediately began to manhandle him. He fought back, putting three policemen in hospital. Suddenly a siege had started which went on for hours. The police sent dogs into Obedyne's flat only to find them being flung out again with knife wounds. He was eventually overpowered by their sheer weight of numbers.

He was sentenced to fourteen years for the attacks on the policemen and their dogs. By the time he arrived at the prison he was like a wounded lion. He just wanted to get his own back on the authorities. I was in Wandsworth Prison when they first brought him there and, as usual, I was in the punishment block. It wasn't long before I realized that they had someone in the block who was giving them plenty to think about. I knew he was black by the racist remarks that were being screamed at him.

That's all I knew at that time but I soon heard the stories that were going around the jail of this enormous Nigerian, with immense strength, who refused to give in when they were beating him up.

We had both been in the punishment block at Dartmoor for quite some time, but had never met because of the requirements of segregation and solitary confinement. You would be locked in your cell all day long. There were three or four cages at the back of the cells which were used for exercise purposes. The only time you came out of your cell was to go into the cage for about half an hour a day. So it wasn't until I came out of the punishment block that I first met Obedyne.

The circumstances of that first meeting were very strange because the authorities decided to put Obedyne and myself to work together! I will never be able to fathom the reasoning behind the move but I don't think the result was what they were hoping for. Although Obedyne had come from the punishment block they still kept him segregated from the rest of the prisoners and put him to work in the wood-shed. There he sat on a wooden bench with a chopping block in front of him and an axe. He was expected to chop sticks for the screws' fires whilst we were all freezing to death in our cells. I was seen by the Governor a few weeks after Obedyne was put to work in the wood-shed and told that I was going to be let out of the punishment cells. The Home Office had decided that I was to work on my own for a while, but they already had a man on restricted association at work. The result was that Obedyne and myself were put together to do our tasks.

The next morning a screw came for myself and Obedyne. We went to the Chief's office, where he signed for a flat wooden box, and were then taken to the wood-shed. The working arrangements had already been sorted out. There were now two wooden benches to sit on, one opposite the other, both with a chopping block in front of them. Obedyne sat on one bench, I sat on the other and then the screw just slid the box into the middle of the floor between us. We looked down and saw two axes lying neatly in the box.

We both took an axe apiece and started looking at each other. It was deadly silent in the wood-shed. We both stared at the screw who appeared to be on the verge of a heart attack. Obedyne turned his gaze back to me and said, 'I like you, I no like him,' pointing at the screw. I agreed with him. We then started to play little games like chopping quickly at the block of wood to make the sticks fly towards the screw's chair. Within a few days his nerve had gone completely. I was sitting in my cell reading, whilst the evening association privileges were going on, when the door opened. It was the screw, practically shaking from head to foot.

He said, 'I want to make a deal with you. If Obedyne ever attacks either you or me, if you help me, I'll give evidence that you saved my life.'

I just looked at him and thought of all the times that those people had me helpless in the body belt or strait-jacket and not once had there ever been the slightest mercy shown. I just got back to my book and didn't even answer him.

I never saw him again, but within a few days the new wood-shed party had been disbanded and they put Obedyne in the laundry and me back into the quarry.

Although my attitude to most of the screws never changed, a sort of truce was gradually established. I remember sitting in the mat shop one day, not doing any work, just looking at the screw who was sitting by the alarm bell. Immediately behind him was a guy called

Pierre, who was located a few cells from me. Pierre was enormous in stature and came from Trinidad. One day he approached me and asked, 'Why don't they make you work?'

'Well,' I said, 'it goes back many years, you see. I used to clash with the authorities but now we've kind of called a draw, so they don't bother me and I don't bother them.'

He started to tell me how hard he found it to do the job. His hands were so big that he found it very difficult to keep taking the coir around the ropes suspended on the frame and his fingers were red raw. I said, 'I know, I've done plenty of that in the past but now I don't do it.'

The next day in the workshop Pierre just sat there doing no work, until one of the discipline screws noticed and started to remonstrate with him. The next thing the screw saw was a hospital ward when he finally regained consciousness after the terrible hiding Pierre had given him. I didn't see Pierre for a few months and when I did meet him again he was still getting over the beating they had given him. But he had a different job and he seemed to have settled into it. He could just manage a grin when he said, 'At least they never put me back in the mat shop.'

One guy I felt particularly sorry for in Dartmoor was doing life for killing his wife. His name was Robbie and he had been sentenced to death in the Channel Islands, then been reprieved and sent to the mainland to do his life sentence. Apparently, there was a rule that a guy couldn't be released on licence, to the Channel Islands, unless he had someone to sign and be responsible for him, which Robbie didn't have. He had been sentenced in the thirties and by the time I first saw him in the fifties he weighed about six stone and had been sewing mail bags for fourteen years. He always looked freezing and hungry and when the new boiler house was built, and we got central heating pipes in the cell blocks, Robbie would rush into the wing after work and wrap himself around an upright pipe in the corner of D Wing. It became known as Robbie's Corner. I remember the Salvation Army campaigning for his release and after about twenty-five years they eventually gained his freedom. He hadn't seen any of the War and, as there were no newspapers or radios in prison in those days, he didn't know much about life outside. He was a little scared of going out and seeing the speed of cars and such things. I heard later that he died about two months after his release.

Perhaps some of the most interesting people in Dartmoor in those days were the quiet guys. One, in particular, was Rubber Bones Webb. You wouldn't have given him a second glance but all the same he pulled off one of the greatest prison escapes of all time. The fact that he was on special watch as a potential escapee made his feat even more outstanding.

When Rubber Bones decided to escape, through an air vent that ran under his cell, he studied every detail of the screws' actions, when they did their bolts and bars check, which in the case of a special watch prisoner was very frequent. He noticed that regardless of who did the checking, there was one part of the cell that they never stood on. It was just off centre on a straight line to the bars on the window; they only checked the outside wall and window as the potential escapee would still be in the cell block if he dug in any other place. They knew it was practically impossible to go through the walls because, unlike most prisons, Dartmoor's walls had been built by French prisoners of war using solid rock hewn from the quarry. However, Rubber Bones had noticed, whilst in the exercise yard, that there was a grille about eighteen inches by nine inches with a large lock on it, situated just about three feet below his cell. There had to be an air shaft of some description.

Rubber Bones quickly went into action. He first needed to enlist the help of a couple of trusted men because as he was on special watch he never came out of his cell on association. Association worked to a set of established rules. If a prisoner was on second-stage, that is after doing eighteen months of his sentence, he was allowed two one-hour periods out of his cell per week. If he was on third-stage, after doing two and a half years of his sentence, he was allowed three evening periods per week.

Rubber Bones recruited a man from each association period to sit near his cell while he dug down to the air shaft. The floor was covered with a bitumen-like material that most cons polished with the wax that was used on the threads we sewed the mail bags with. Each period Rubber Bones would take the cover, which he had made with the help of a chap in the carpentry shop, from the hole he was digging and each evening he would replace the cover and then polish it to match the rest of his floor. He got rid of the stuff he was digging up – mainly sand – by dribbling it through his trousers on to the exercise yard which was a rough stony area directly outside D Wing. A couple of his friends would get rid of the stuff in the same way. Dartmoor having the type of weather it does, every prisoner was issued with a heavy waterproof coat which made it easy to conceal a fair bit of the sand. It was a painstaking and nerve-racking operation but the delight when he eventually hit the air shaft could be seen in his demeanour as he went to and from work.

But the really hard part was still to come. He knew the air shaft was too narrow to get through with clothes on, so he would have to rely on the guys giving up their meagre margarine ration to rub on to his body when he was ready to go. However, the real stumbling block was the problem of how to get the lock off the grid on the outside, once he'd gone head first down the shaft, as there would be no coming back at that point. Eventually, one of his friends acquired a steel bar, like a jemmy, from the tool bag of one of the civilian maintenance staff.

At last Rubber Bones was ready to go. He waited for the first check after lights out (he would then have a half light in his cell, as did all special watch prisoners). He set up a lifelike dummy in his bed, stripped completely naked and smeared himself with the complete margarine ration of about ten cons for the week. Then, pushing his small bundle of clothes in front, he proceeded head first down the hole. It took him about one and a half hours to get to and bust the lock on the grid. Once outside D Wing, he made his way to the builder's yard inside the prison, snapped the lock with his jemmy and helped himself to a ladder. Within minutes he was over the wall.

He knew that, given a fair bit of luck, he would have about four hours before they missed him, so instead of going over the moors – which had been the downfall of many potential escapees, such as Billy Day who died in the bogs when he escaped with Dennis Stafford – he decided to go by road via Okehampton. When the boys in the 'Moor knew that he'd arrived in London, there were a lot of smiling faces walking around the exercise yard, even though everyone knew that there would be extra bread and water dished out over the next few months for any number of trivial offences.

There was one guy in Dartmoor who never smiled at anything. He was always very deep and I wasn't surprised to read, years after he had finished a life sentence, that he had been re-arrested and charged with molesting little girls at a hotel where he worked. His name was James Camb and he was serving a life sentence at Dartmoor for one of the most celebrated murder cases after the Second World War. It was known as the Porthole Murder Mystery. James Camb was a steward on one of the big ocean liners. On this liner was a very attractive actress returning to Britain from South Africa. When the journey was halfway completed it was discovered that the actress had disappeared, and when the ship docked the police went aboard and questioned certain members of the crew. Eventually Camb was arrested and, after a sensational trial at the Old Bailey, was found guilty and sentenced to death. He was later reprieved and served a life sentence instead. Many chaps in Dartmoor tried to discover from Camb whether he'd killed her and pushed her through the porthole but his eyes just glazed over and he refused to talk about it.

I remember one incident in the 'Moor that gave all the guys in my wing a little bit of light relief. We had an old screw on our landing who got on well with everyone, never bothered putting people on report and just did his job.

Most people were glad to see him come on to the landing at unlocking time. One night I was listening in my cell to a radio programme that featured a 'mystery voice challenge'. When the mystery voice came on I immediately recognized it as belonging to an old pal of mine who had been in the nick with me years before. Since getting out of prison in the fifties he had become a successful writer. His first book *Bang to Rights* was very amusing, about all of the characters he had met in jail. Years later when I met him, in his old haunts in Soho, I couldn't believe it was the same Frank Norman. His voice was now much plummier, except on the odd occasion after we'd had a few drinks in the Colony club. So when I came out of my cell in the morning, knowing that a lot of chaps tried to guess the mystery voice, I said, 'Did any of you recognize the voice?'

No one did and they all thought it would go to the maximum prize of £100. I approached the old screw and said, 'Get your wife to listen in and send a card to enter, and when they ask the name say it's Frank Norman the author.'

The competition seemed to go on for weeks. Each night all of the cons on our landing would sit up and wait for them to phone the three contestants, and eventually the prize reached the magic £100. Every night the old screw would come in and say, 'The missus is still waiting for the call.'

Finally the night came when the presenter said, 'We are calling a contestant in Princetown.' We all listened attentively and sure enough it was the screw's wife. When asked what she did she said, 'I'm the wife of a prison warder in

Dartmoor.' Then when she said who she thought the mystery voice was, the presenter got excited and said, 'Yes, you're right!'

A big cheer went up around the cell block. Then the presenter asked, 'How did you guess the name?'

'Frank Norman's friend is doing time in my husband's landing,' she said.

'Will you be sharing the £100 with the prisoner?' he asked.

'Oh no! I'm not allowed to do that but my husband will probably give him and his mates a bit of tobacco – but don't tell anyone,' she replied.

Her husband nearly got the sack over that.

Violence had become a part of our daily life and not just the violence between screw and prisoner. More often it was between prisoners themselves. Most cons in Dartmoor carried a weapon and nearly every day someone was attacked. The situation came to a head in the chapel in the beginning of the sixties. It was a Sunday afternoon and we were all going to a picture show entitled *The Blue Lamp*, a drama about a policeman being murdered. A few days earlier a friend of mine, Cyril Birkett, had been charged with attacking another prisoner and two other cons had given evidence against him. To inform against another inmate was one of the worst offences in the eyes of your fellow cons and it was normal to put a 'mark' on the offender. This sort of justice seemed entirely natural to us – we had our own rules that we lived by.

When it was seen that one of the grasses was lining up

to go to the pictures it was decided that he would be attacked when the lights went out. It wasn't hard to arrange to sit behind the victim as all one had to do was to be the eighteenth person after him when going into the chapel. In this way you would be seated immediately behind the guy concerned. Dennis Thirkettle, another friend of Cyril's on our landing, placed himself in the relevant position, with me next to him.

The film started, the lights went out and everyone settled down to watch. The film had not been rolling long when I heard a cry of pain from the man just in front of us. He stood up and I could see his silhouette against the screen as he pulled a knife from his back. He turned and lunged at Dennis. The knife went straight into Dennis's heart. I immediately wrapped my jacket around my arm. As the lights went on again I threw it up in front of the guy with the knife and knocked him to the floor. Prisoners were scrambling over the pews to get out of the way and I was fighting with a couple of screws who'd seen me knock down the con who stabbed Dennis. Everyone seemed to have decided to settle their differences, myself included, and the result was mayhem.

The screws decided to make a quick retreat so they ran out leaving the doors open. This was a sign for everyone to get out, quickly. There was one man lying dead and about twenty others injured. Within minutes prisoners were hurrying back to their cells, hoping they hadn't been noticed in the chapel. During the confusion four of us decided to raid the kitchen as we knew it would be a long time before we got another meal. We helped ourselves to as much grub as we could carry and returned to our cells.

It was about six in the evening when the screws came for us and they had the police with them. They took six of us to the punishment block and over the next month the police tried to piece together a case. Eventually the trial came up at Exeter Assizes and everyone was found not guilty. After a period of time in the punishment block the Home Office decided to split us all up. I was sent to Walton Prison in Liverpool, where I was to meet up with a lot of old friends including Jack McVitie. Tommy Flanagan went to Winson Green, Birmingham and Donnie Adams went to Strangeways, Manchester.

On arriving at Liverpool I was taken immediately to the punishment block, in H Wing. The next morning the Governor and his merry men came to the cell and informed me that, as I still had a couple more years to go of my sentence, it had been decided by the Home Office that I would be kept in solitary confinement for the duration. This was stated as being in the interests of maintaining good order and discipline within the prison. However, the Governor relented after a short period and allowed me into the prison proper. I was left to get on with my time without any problems whatsoever and I could come and go as I wanted to. My old friend from my early days at Dartmoor, Mixie Walsh, used to visit me from Blackpool where he lived.

Walton Prison at this time had just come through a major shake-up as a result of the actions of a remarkable lady MP, Bessie Braddock. Her enquiries and determination led to the exposure of the brutality that had been going on at the prison. Many prison warders had been charged, some were given a short prison sentence and many others were disciplined. The dust had only just settled when I got there.

There were a few screws who had avoided punishment, and these were among the ringleaders of the heavy mob. Jack the Hat, who had been transferred to Liverpool from another prison because of his bad behaviour, took an instant dislike to one of them. Jack would taunt him about his reputation as a bully and challenge him to come to Jack's cell and 'fight like a man'. The screw was unable to oblige as he was still under a cloud after the Braddock enquiry and Jack became very popular with the other cons for keeping him in his place.

Like Jack I had a bit of a reputation myself, though the reaction of other cons was not always what it seemed. One day a fellow inmate came up to me and said, 'Are you the guy that had the cat-o'-nine-tails?' I nodded and he started to ask me what it was like and would I describe it to him. As I obliged I noticed his eyes becoming glazed. When I told Jack about him, he laughed and said, 'Didn't you know that he was a school master and used to get all the sixth-formers to beat him with the cane. He's having the time of his life talking to you about being flogged.'

Although I was still inside I was aware of what was going on in the lives of the Krays. When Reggie and I were in Wandsworth, while we were working or walking in the exercise yard we'd talk about our plans for the future. I didn't want to go back to crime when I got out and Reggie said he and Ronnie would help me set up my own business. The only business we were interested in was nightclubs. Nightclub bosses seemed to have a glamour about them, with a bit of shadiness that appealed to people like us.

After Ronnie had been discharged he and Charlie used to come up to visit Reggie and myself. A little while after Reggie had been released Frank Mitchell and myself were told that the Home Office had stopped any future visits from the Kray family. I'd just received a visit from Reggie at Dartmoor when, shortly afterwards, a guy who was a quite well-known prisoner put himself on protection. He must have realized that Reggie had told me how this guy had tried to fit him up many years before. In fact Reggie had told me, but he wasn't vindictive about it, he even made excuses for the guy by saying, 'He was only young in those days and he didn't know any better.' I never found Reggie a vindictive person. It was a well known fact in the East End that if you'd upset the twins, you could always go and have a word with Reggie and he'd calm Ronnie down.

Although life outside prison seemed very far away, Reggie kept me informed of all the news in the letters he used to write me. I've always kept his letters and reading through them now I realize that Reggie looked on life as one big merry-go-round. He had a very good sense of humour. In one letter he mentions someone who 'broke Tony's jaw the other day. The guy who did it was the guy who left you a tin of syrup when he went out.' This was a coded message from Reggie who was referring to himself. In this way he let me know that the Krays were taking over Tony Snyder's rackets.

During the time I was in Dartmoor the twins had started to get friendly with people from America. Frank Sinatra's son, Frank Jr., had been kidnapped and soon afterwards he did a tour of Great Britain. As a result of the earlier incident it was arranged that his minders would accompany him. A couple of guys came over with him, one of whom, Eddie Pucci, I met later in Stockholm. The twins were also contacted to make sure Frank Jr. had no problems. So by the time I was released from prison the twins were well on their way in every respect. They were making plenty of money, had plenty of friends and not too many enemies. Most of the celebrities, on both sides of the Atlantic, liked to be in their company.

My own view is that the twins never set out to become gang bosses, as a lot of people think. It was something that just happened as a natural consequence of the fact that they were both very likeable personalities and also known to be very tough. They attracted people to them and they were heroes to a lot of guys.

Charlie at this time was dabbling in the world of pop group management, had a nice recording studio and dance club in partnership with the Clark brothers, the American dancers. On the morning of my release from Liverpool Mixie Walsh and Steve and Jimmy Clark picked me up. The twins had asked the two brothers to collect me and had sent a few quid as a coming home present. That was a wonderful day, one that I thought many times I would not see. I didn't get back to London until the next day as Mixie and a few of his friends had laid on a big party in a club in Preston owned by Joe Lancaster, a chap I was to become very friendly with a year or so later. I promised to return and visit them after I got settled in London.

CHAPTER THIRTEEN

West End Club Owner and the 'Firm'

After celebrating my home coming with my friends in Blackpool I caught the train down to London. I was met by 'Duke' Osbourne who I'd met during my early days in prison and who had been a friend of mine now for many years. He had a great personality, was tall and slim and always had a smile on his face. He was into every racket that he could find, both in prison and out. He was always the prison 'baron' as well as being the prison bookmaker. I believe he ended up getting into drug smuggling and was wanted for this when he was found dead under strange circumstances, probably drug-related.

Duke was also a very good friend of Reggie and Ronnie Kray so as soon as I stepped off the train we went immediately to 178 Vallance Road where the twins lived at that time with their mother Violet. It was one of a small block of terraced houses in Bethnal Green and had become the meeting place for all of the firm. Everyone was very well mannered and respectful when they visited Vallance Road, mainly because the twins' mother was always in the house. She was a really nice person. She always had tea and sandwiches on the go and would bring them into the little front room where the twins held their meetings.

The twins arranged for us to have another celebration at the Cambridge Rooms that night, so I could meet members of the firm that I didn't already know. The twins by this time had many and varied business interests and Reggie had also married Frances, a girl he used to tell me about in his letters. When we arrived at the Cambridge Rooms it was packed with guys who, in one way or another, had an interest with the twins. Whther it was in the best interest of the twins or not is another matter.

One of the guys there that evening was called Les Payne who seemed to have a fair amount of influence over Reg and Ron. He was always trying to involve them in his wild money-making schemes and, I believe, was mainly interested in using them for his own good. Eventually he realized that they were getting wise to him and he was the one who finally helped the police nail them. He wrote a book about the twins and his activities called *The Brotherhood*.

Also there that night was Teddy Smith, who I first met in Wandsworth and had introduced to the twins a few years earlier. I bumped into him later at the Colony club where he introduced me to one of the greatest characters I ever met – Francis Bacon. Although Ted was close to the twins I think he would like to get away now and then to be with his artistic friends and every so often he would say to me, 'Do you fancy a drink in Soho?'

Most of the original members of the firm were there – Micky Forsyth, Johnny Davis, Terry O'Brian, Dicky Morgan and Curly King. I also met Stubby Kaye, an American actor who had appeared in *Guys and Dolls*, and Terry Spinks, ex-Olympic gold medallist, both of whom liked to socialize with the twins.

Everyone seemed to be friendly and enjoying themselves – even the bookmakers and publicans who used to help financially seemed happy. I knew many of the people in the company but as I'd been away a few years there were a lot of new faces on the firm. However everyone was, as always, very polite and it was a good evening.

The cabaret act that night was a very good singer called Lennie Peters, who remained a good friend of mine until his recent death. This was before Lennie had met Diane Lee to become Peters and Lee. Lennie was always a good friend to the people who tried to help him and he kept in touch with Reggie and Ronnie. We used to meet now and again and chat about the old days over a couple of drinks. He was one of the very few people who never changed over the years and he had the same old sense of humour. We often mentioned his early days in the East End when he had a partner, Brian 'Butch' Royal, who was another great singer. They used to sing at the Greengate in Bethnal Green Road and all the firm would pop in to catch the show. Those were marvellous days. You would never know who would turn up to have a drink and a chat with the boys and listen to the music, even get on stage to play along with Lennie and Butch. One particular night a girl called Winifred Atwell, who was a big star in those days and a brilliant pianist, came down to perform on stage with Lennie and we all ended up going back to her flat in Mayfair after the show. She was rather intrigued by all these smart young men with their nice cars and ready cash. Quite innocently she remarked, 'You're all obviously from good families.'

Shortly after coming home in 1963 I became the proprietor of the Emerald Beach club in Soho. It was a basement premises that had become very popular and I heard, from a friend I'd met in Dartmoor, that the owner was having trouble with some local heavies. My friend was sure that the owner would offer me the business for a nominal rent which indeed is what happened. Then Maurice King, who was the proprietor of the Starlite club, was offered the Brown Derby club for a very reasonable price. He'd heard of my success with the Emerald Beach and came to me with an offer of a partnership in the Brown Derby, thereby ensuring himself protection in the Starlite for no cost. I ran both clubs myself, with some excellent staff, and loved the lifestyle. Comparing it to my previous way of life, I think this was my idea of going straight!

Maurice had a very thriving business in the pop world. He managed quite a few of the stars of the day including Shirley Bassey's affairs and those of Jackie Trent. Quite a few of the successful bands of the sixties, the Walker Brothers and the Rockin' Berries, were on his books. Maurice rarely came over to the Brown Derby. His headquarters were at the Starlite club in Stratford Place, Oxford Street. But if ever he got any problems with hard-case customers he would give me a ring as it would only take me a few minutes to pop over. It was an ideal partnership. If Maurice had any customers who wanted to go into Soho and look at the shady side of life he would call me and ask me to keep an eye on them. Consequently, I would end up with a pretty mixed clientele of villains, sporting personalities and pop singers plus all of the people such types seemed to attract.

One of the nicest people who would always look in, if he

was in the West End, was Terry Murphy, who would be accompanied by a couple of ex-fighters and business associates. I was always pleased to see Terry and his friends as they were the tops as far as drinking customers went. Terry had been one of the best middleweight fighters in the country in the fifties. His fight with Lew Lazar for the southern area middleweight title was the first fight to be televised on the independent network. I had some great nights out with Terry and his friends, one of whom was Terry Spinks.

One evening we were in the Mayfair Hotel having a nice drink and it was getting late. One member of our party was having difficulty finding the toilet. He was getting desperate when he noticed a tropical stream which was part of the decor, complete with palm trees and real crocodiles. He decided to have a quick wee into the stream which was nearly the biggest mistake of his life as the crocs were not too pleased with our friend relieving himself on top of them. I don't think the management were too happy either.

I think the boys I became closer to than any others in the business were the Rockin' Berries. Clive Lee, Terry Bond, Chuck Bottfield and Jeff Turton, from the original band, were perhaps my particular friends in those days. Both Terry and Chuck came to visit me whilst I was in prison. I have seen them all at different times over the years. Chuck was the only one of the original Berries left when I last saw them but I saw quite a lot of Clive after he took over from Russ Abbott to front the Black Abbots.

A year or so ago I was in Jersey on business and took six Chinese friends along. We had all been out to dinner and decided to go out to a nightclub to end the evening. The hotel porter told us there was a nice club called Ryders just fifty yards from the hotel. So myself and three of my friends went along there. It was getting late and there was no one on the door. We walked in and followed the sound of the music until we found ourselves in the club bar. I was looking for someone to introduce ourselves to when I heard a voice say, 'I don't believe it, is that you, Eric?' It was Terry Bond, the ex-drummer of the Rockin' Berries, and he was the governor of the place. It was a very pleasant surprise. We swapped a few stories that night and all went back for dinner the following evening. We had a really nice time.

One of the hardest days I ever had with that lot was when we promoted a show at Sofia Gardens in Cardiff. P.J. Proby was topping the bill with the Berries and a few other bands. The front guy was one of the most outrageous characters I've ever met in my life. He was a lovely guy called Tony Marsh and was, in his day, Britain's number one DJ. Maurice phoned me the night before the show and said, 'Eric, for God's sake don't let Proby and Tony get near the booze before the show.'

'Don't worry, Maurice, I'll stick to them like glue,' I promised.

I thought I'd done a good job but when we got to Cardiff, Proby nearly fell out of the car and Tony had a big grin on his face. As I'd been driving those two had slipped a bottle out of a holdall in the back seat and finished it off. All was well in the end, although I nearly had a fit when Proby almost fell off the stage. However, his voice carried him through. It's sad when a guy with such talent falls from grace.

Tony Marsh had a bit of a traumatic life in the business as he was always clashing with the powers that be and got into more than one scrape. The most noticeable one came when he was introducing the Rolling Stones on stage at Slough. He dashed off stage and was changing in the wings when he realized a lot of the audience could see him with no trousers on. He was in fact charged with indecent exposure and fined £25. The incident all but finished his career.

I remember throwing a party for the Dreamers, the boys that backed Freddy Garrity. They had just done a concert at Hammersmith, with the Beatles, and were then off to America. We had the party as a good luck send off. On stage, at the Starlite, were four top rock and roll bands. Every few minutes another face walked into the club. Eric Burdon, of the Animals, came in with a guy no one had heard of in those days and Eric asked if the kid could do a spot. With a request from someone like Eric Burdon the kid was soon on stage. He was incredible, his name was Steve Marriot. Tom Jones turned up with the drummer from his band the Squires. Elkie Brooks was also there I remember. She was about fifteen in those days and she still remains one of my favourite singers. It was an incredible night. Ray Davis and the Kinks, Jackie Trent, P.J. Proby and many other musicians turned up, a tribute to the popularity of the Dreamers. We also got some gate crashers who started to pester people and made a nuisance of themselves. Speaking into the mike one of the boys in the band told them to leave in no uncertain terms. To show that if you give a dog a bad name it sticks, one of the well-known music papers of the day ran a story about the evening. In the article it enquires, 'Who was the delightful chap who told the gate crashers to fuck off? Was it Tony Marsh?' Poor old Tony, he got the blame for starting everything in those days.

I used to see Reggie Kray every day and in the evenings we would go out together into the West End, usually ending up either in the Stork club or some similar establishment. One place we used to pop into quite frequently was the Flamingo in Wardour Street which quite a few of the superstars of the present day used to frequent. Long John Baldry was the name in those days and he used to play there quite often as did Georgie Fame and the Blue Flames. But it was the kids who used to hang around there, hoping to make it some day, who were the ones that stood out. And they certainly did that. I love the music of some of those kids, who are not kids any more, such as Elton John and Rod Stewart. The boss of the Flamingo was a guy called Rick Gunnell and he loved to introduce Reggie as his pal to the various 'faces' that frequented the club.

It was around this time that I was sitting in a club that I used to frequent quite often, with a couple of friends enjoying a quiet drink. There were also a few people we recognized as a party from another firm. Oliver Reed, who was with some friends, upset the party that was sitting a few yards from us and one of the guys smashed a glass into his face. We hustled the guys, who wanted to smash the place up, out of the club and went to look at him. There was a lot of blood about and one or two bad cuts but he didn't make too much fuss about it. This episode didn't seem to do his career any harm. In fact the scars could have enhanced his reputation!

It was around this time that Reggie and myself went to Stockholm with another friend called Johnny Squibby. Johnny was a very amusing guy, full of fun and practical jokes. We were sitting in the plane at Heathrow just before take-off and Reggie had already admitted his dislike of flying and had downed a few large brandies before boarding, when John started his non-stop banter. 'I'm sorry we've got this type of plane as it's got the worst record of all for crashing,' he informed us.

Then, after we had taken off it was, 'Can you hear that funny noise coming from the engine . . .?'

Reggie nearly exploded. 'The only noise I can hear is coming out of your mouth, so just button up.'

We had to change at Copenhagen and Squibby was larking about in the duty-free, when Reggie said desperately, 'I can't stand much more of this. Is there a boat we can get on?'

We eventually landed in Stockholm and went straight to the Grand Hotel where Frank Sinatra had the whole of the floor above us booked for his entourage. In Sinatra's company were a couple of minders who had come to England with Frank Jr. and it was one of these, Eddie Pucci, who'd phoned Reggie inviting him to Stockholm to meet Frank and a few other people. They would all be there for the boxing between Floyd Patterson and Eddie Machin and, as there were a few British fighters on the same bill, it would be an ideal meeting place.

It wasn't long after we booked in that Eddie Pucci phoned our suite to let us know what was happening. As there were a lot of press people about we would have a proper meeting later. We were to meet at the weigh-in and later have dinner at the Flamingo Hotel after the fights. As we had planned a week's stay in Stockholm we decided we'd go and give the town the once over on the first night. We had a superb night, met some nice people and found the girls very friendly. Reggie was always shy in front of women but they found him very attractive.

The next morning, a Sunday, we went to the weigh-in at a nightclub called the Ambassador, in Kingsgarten. As we walked in, the place was packed and on the stage were all of the American crowd plus a couple of English fight managers, Denny Mancini and Johnny Campbell. Both had fighters on the bill. We went straight to the stage where we were greeted by everyone. In the American contingent was Nat Fleicher, editor of *The Ring* magazine. I'd met him when he came with Rocky Marciano and Al Weil to England and they visited the prison I was in at the time. Some of those involved in the American boxing world of the fifties and sixties had links with organized crime, due partly to the practice of rigging fights. So Nat was thrilled to find himself chatting away about the British penal system with a top criminal on the stage of a night club in the Swedish capital.

When it came to fight time, scheduled for the afternoon, the word went out that Sinatra wasn't well and wouldn't be attending so would friends from London like to use the seats. Everyone in the place was watching the seat with Sinatra's name on it. When we arrived and Reggie sat in Sinatra's chair he was nearly mobbed by dozens of girls who then sat at his feet throughout the fights. Between fights all the local celebrities came over to shake hands. I'm not sure whether they thought we were in Sinatra's company or were the 'men from London' as everyone referred to us. Ingmar Johanson, who was the ex-heavyweight champion of the world, joined us and was very charming but I could tell by his conversation that he didn't know who we were.

Later that evening we went to dinner at the Flamingo where we were joined by Johnny Campbell, his fighter Ray Sheil and a bookmaker friend Burt Ashman. I was to meet Ashman again years later when I was involved in a big betting coup. This was supposed to be Frank Sinatra's dinner but he was the only person who didn't attend. Later that night we were taken to Burns nightclub to meet Sinatra and his friends. One in particular who I enjoyed meeting was Van Heflin, the film actor, who was very good company. Sinatra was very impressive. He was the perfect host. Everything was noticed and no one's glass was left empty at any time. It was a memorable night. In fact, we had another five days after that. It was one of the most enjoyable weeks I ever had. But our visit to Stockholm came to an end and we returned to London.

Both the twins and Charlie were frequent visitors to the Emerald Beach and the Brown Derby. It was on one of these visits to the Brown Derby that they met Maurice King. Whilst I was having a drink with Reggie and Ronnie the phone rang and it was Maurice who seemed rather agitated about some customers who were giving a bit of trouble. I told Maurice I'd get over straight away and then said to Reggie, 'I've got to pop over to the Starlite for a few minutes.'

Reggie said, 'We'll come over with you.'

I could see they fancied a change of venue and they'd

never been to the Starlite before so I said, 'I might have to "talk" to a couple of people over there and then we can have a nice drink.'

Once we arrived at the Starlite there was no problem as the people who had been causing the aggravation had already left in rather a hurry as I understand it. We settled down for a pleasant evening.

At this time the twins were doing business with Dino Cellini, who had brought George Raft from America to front the Colony Casino club. Dino had an interest in quite a few other clubs in London and the twins were 'on wages' to see there was no trouble. Whilst we were chatting to Maurice in the Starlite club it was mentioned that there was plenty of room for gaming tables in the club. Within a few weeks a casino was set up and everyone was happy. Dino's staff were running the show, Maurice was getting his rent plus the extra clientele and the twins were having their few quid. But one night there was a slight hiccup.

I used to pop into the Starlite most evenings and on this particular evening I looked in, as usual, on my way to the Astor Club in Berkeley Square for a late dinner. Whilst in the Starlite I had a drink at the bar and mentioned that I was on my way to the Astor and said goodnight. I'd no sooner sat down in the Astor when Sulki, the manager, came over to me and said, 'You're wanted on the phone urgently.' I went to the office right away and it was one of the barmaids from the Starlite, sounding distressed and saying, 'Eric, we've been stuck up by four gunmen and robbed. They've taken everything. They've made everyone take their clothes off, taken all the money from the casino and gone with the punters' clothes, wallets, handbags and jewellery.' She said one of the customers had phoned the police.

I said, 'Phone Maurice and tell him to get down there straight away and when the law have finished with you come to the Astor.'

I then phoned the twins who were not very amused. 'Who would do this to us? They've got to be found. We can't have the word going round that people have robbed us! See what you can find out,' they said.

Well, I did find out, many years later, when I was sitting with a couple of chaps planning a bank job and they started to laugh and mentioned the Starlite robbery. They recalled the circumstances. They had just pulled up ready to go in to hold the place up when I arrived and walked into the club. They decided to wait until after I'd left as they knew that I wouldn't be too long. But I had stopped to talk to the barmaid and I was a bit longer than I normally would have been. So there were four chaps sitting outside the club, with shotguns, waiting for me to leave before they would go in! To this day I think I'm the only person who knows the identity of the chaps who robbed the Starlite.

In the mean time I had been introduced to Peter Rachmann who the twins did some business with. Rachmann was a Polish Jew who had suffered in the Warsaw ghetto and in a concentration camp and had learned to be a survivor at a very early age. He landed in this country just after the War, when he was in his twenties, he acquired a sizeable fortune from developing slum properties and his methods of getting sitting tenants out of their flats left much to be desired. When I knew him he lived in a mansion in Hampstead's 'millionaires' row' and was just starting to get fat. He still had a very charming manner and women found him fascinating. His girlfriend at the time was Mandy Rice-Davis. He surrounded himself with heavy guys, mainly ex-boxers and wrestlers, and could often be seen at the Cumberland or Regent Palace Hotels where there was a carvery offering as much as you could eat for £2.10. It was a sight to see Rachmann and about five or six giant ex-fighters tucking in to everything in sight. They'd go through a leg of lamb, a joint of beef – or pork for the non-Jews – heaps of potatoes and vegetables and then tuck in to mounds of cheesecakes and trifles. Rachmann died in Edgeware General Hospital about twenty years ago from dissipation. I believe they had to cut all of the gold from his wrists and fingers because he had become so fat. One of Rachmann's managers, Lenny Royal, gave me a lovely flat in Kensington rent free. I had a name for myself after being flogged in Wandsworth and was known for my battles with authority. That kind of reputation meant something to men like Rachmann – by giving me a flat he neutralized someone who might be a threat to him and had the added bonus of being able to point me out as a 'friend', showing that he knew some heavy people.

At the end of '63 I got the Beach club in Gerard Place and the twins would come at least once a week and bring all of the firm. I still used to spend most of my days with the twins but I saw a lot more of Reggie than I did of Ronnie. They liked to have their own friends and get away from each other for short periods, just for a bit of breathing space. Whenever we met in the evenings it was now invariably in the Grave Maurice or the Widows. The twins would always be together.

There was a very unfortunate incident one night when we were all to meet at the La Monde in King's Road, Chelsea. The club was run by one of the twins' oldest friends, George Osborne. The meeting had been arranged for that evening at Ossie's and everyone had been invited. In the end there were about twenty of us awaiting George's arrival. But no George. So Ronnie enquired politely, 'George is late coming down to greet us?'

A girl serving behind the bar, who happened to be George's step-daughter, said in a matter-of-fact voice, 'George won't be coming tonight. He and my mum have decided to stay in.'

The girl's attitude didn't help to put Ronnie in a better mood, and suddenly he said, 'Get that arsehole on the phone.'

After Reggie and Ronnie had had a bit of a row and Charlie had tried to calm things down, the girl got Ossie on the phone. By this time Ronnie was beside himself with rage. He grabbed the phone and started to scream at Ossie: 'You ungrateful bastard. We've given you everything you've got and now you're over here with your poncy Chelsea friends you want to blank your old mates. So keep your ear on the phone and you can listen to what's going to happen to your lovely little club.'

With that he turned to the few regulars who were in there and said, 'Just sit where you are, don't move and you won't get hurt.'

Taking a soda syphon he smashed all the mirrors and optics behind the bar. Then he systematically smashed the rest of the club up without anyone saying a word. When he finished he picked up the phone and said, 'We're going off to drink with real people.' And we all got in our cars and went off to another club.

The next morning Reggie phoned me and said, 'Will you come over to Vallance Road right away?'

When I got there Reggie, Ronnie and Charlie were sitting in the front room of the house looking very serious. Ronnie was down in the dumps and he asked if I thought what he'd done was right. I told him, being diplomatic, that in a way it was right. This seemed to brighten him up a little. But then I said, 'You can't really blame George, he's now married to the lady and she obviously has a lot of influence over him. He definitely wouldn't snub you. He thinks too much of you.' With this Ronnie, tears coming in to his eyes, said, 'Reg, get Ossie on the phone, I want to speak to him.'

He then apologized to Ossie and said, 'Spare no expense, get the club fixed up and send the bill to me.'

Ronnie was a very complex person. Reggie and Charlie were the only two people who could handle him when he was in one of his moods. But he had another side which was charming and humorous. He was also very generous. Ronnie would see an old lady in the street looking as if she had a hard life and would take all the money from his pocket and stuff it in her hands. Money was just something to give away to others – I don't think material things interested him at all. He was happy to live at home with his mum and he only got the flat in Cedra Court so he could entertain his own friends. His generosity got him into an embarassing situation once when I was at Vallance Road. The rest of the family were at the shops and when the milkman called round Ronnie, who'd given all his money away again, was unable to pay him. He walked into the room where I was sitting and, looking deeply uncomfortable, said, 'Will you pay the milkman? I've got no money.' That sort of situation would embarrass Ronnie but I've seen him in a nightclub be handed a bill for a couple of hundred pounds and, without turning a hair, just say that he'd pay next time he was in.

I've enjoyed some good days with him. I was with him and Reggie at Cedra Court, where they both had flats, when Edith Piaf died. Ronnie took it as if it was his own sister who had died and he wanted to go straight to Paris to pay his respects to her.

CHAPTER FIFTEEN

How Organized is the Northern Underworld?

I had by this time acquired a certain amount of knowledge of what was happening in most of the cities in the north of England and any time the twins wanted information concerning the people who ran the nightclub scenes they would give me a ring. So consequently, when Billy Daniels, the famous American singer, phoned from the States to say that he was booked to sing at the Dolce Vita in Newcastle and enquired whether they would be able to see the show Reggie phoned me to ask if I knew someone in Newcastle. I did. I phoned the person I knew and was introduced to the Levy Brothers – David, Marcus and Norman who ran the Dolce Vita.

David Levy said, 'Leave everything to me. Just let me know how many are coming from London and tell me what time the train arrives. I'll do the rest.'

Which he certainly did. There were seven of us and as we stepped out of the station there were two Rolls waiting to take us to the hotel where Billy Daniels was staying. Later the cars came to take us to the club. First the boys showed us around and said there were a few people coming tonight who would like to meet the twins. Reggie and Ronnie were by this time getting quite a reputation all over the country. As the evening progressed we met the guys who ran things in Newcastle in those days. Everyone was very polite to each other, as usual, and we had a wonderful evening. Billy Daniels joined our table after the show and also another guy called Angus Sibbert who ran the one-arm bandit business in that city.

It wasn't long afterwards that Angus Sibbert was gunned down. Two men were later to be given life sentences for his murder. One was a Londoner I knew very well in those days, having met him in Dartmoor where he'd made a dramatic escape with another prisoner who had died in the attempt to get away from the 'Moor. After our visit to Newcastle I bumped into him in London when he said, 'I hear you've been in Newcastle.' I told him we'd only visited socially and he said that he was thinking of settling down up there as he was making a good living. He asked me whether I wanted a bit of the action. I'm glad I refused his kind offer.

Some time later I was in Manchester to visit an old friend of mine and to spend a bit of time getting to know the night life and meet new friends. As I walked into Manchester Piccadilly club, the boss of the casino, Joe Marlow, said to me, 'There's a call from Reggie Kray. He said would you ring him at the Shoreditch number.'

I phoned Reggie that evening and he asked me if I thought the casinos would pay £2,000 to have Joe Louis, the ex-heavyweight champion boxer of the world, appear for a week or £3,000 for two weeks.

I said, 'Leave it with me and I'll call you back in about an hour or so.'

I went back immediately to Joe Marlow and put the

proposition to him but added a monkey to the fee for my own expenses. I knew from experience what it would cost. Joe said the best thing to do would be to go to see Alan Kaye and Gus Denny at the Salford Casino, which we duly did and came away with a two weeks' deal which suited everyone. I relayed this news back to Reggie with the message that it wouldn't do to have too many 'faces' coming to Manchester as the Old Bill were very much on view in the club scene up there.

'No, there'll only be Charlie and a boxing promoter and one of his aides to escort J.L. to Manchester,' Reggie reassured me.

It was decided that I would organize everything in Manchester and we set about the publicity and other arrangements. On the Sunday we had all the press and photographers on parade as the train pulled into Piccadilly station. As flashbulbs exploded around me I stood staring, hardly able to believe my eyes. There, in front of us all, was every top villain in London alighting from the train, smiling happily for the cameras, with Reggie and Ronnie in the forefront.

I hastily gathered them all up and took them immediately to the Midland Hotel to book in. There was a great danger that Joe Louis' appearances would come to an immediate end if the Old Bill knew who was behind bringing him to Manchester. Unfortunately the chaps were determined to go out and give the town the once over and as all of the local villains used the two same clubs it was guaranteed that the Old Bill would be using them too. It was no use thinking we could visit those clubs without the Old Bill tumbling who the strangers were. So we devised the plan of opening the Piccadilly club, which was usually closed on a Sunday, and having a private party. Joe did miracles that night. He only had a few hours to organize everything, to get hold of his regular staff, musicians, doormen, bar staff and kitchen staff. A few of the regulars and a couple of good mates added to the scene and made everything seem like a normal evening in the club.

All was going well until one of the waiters who Ronnie took a shine to, Bertie Burton, who was later to tell the Stalker Inquiry that he was Ronnie's driver, said to Ronnie, 'They've brought us all in to work on our day off to keep you boys happy when there are two very swinging clubs open just around the corner.'

From then on the charade was over. All the chaps wanted to go to one of these clubs and there was no stopping them. We started with the La Petite where there were quite a few entertainers on their night off enjoying life with plenty of pretty girls and one or two local villains, who were obviously put out by the arrival of some obviously very heavy opposition. After a few drinks at the La Petite we went to the Portland Lodge, owned by Bernard Williams, a nice guy who I still see now and again. By this time the word was out as to whose firm was in town, and there were plenty of visitors to the club, some with heavy boots drinking modest halves of bitter, others just rubber necking.

One guy upset Reggie by a remark he made and Reggie duly knocked him out. After this, it was decided that everyone should go back to the Midland Hotel to retire and get together the next morning prior to the twins going back to London. The twins had managed to meet a few club owners and had also sent messages to a couple more to come to the Midland in the morning. There was mention of these particular people giving a few quid to help people who had some problems in London.

The next morning saw us all together. It was a very cosy scene. There was Reggie and Ronnie amiably chatting to a couple of local club owners, with several of the firm sitting about, as well as a few entertainers and friends. I remember Stubby Kaye sitting next to me and a couple of ex-fighters I knew. Suddenly the hotel lounge filled with the Old Bill. Ronnie immediately asked me if I thought I could get out of the hotel without going past the police.

'Yes, I think so,' I said.

He then gave me a packet of money and said, 'Can you bring this down to Vallance Road in a couple of days?'

'Leave it to me,' I said.

I went straight to one of the hotel staff and said, 'You must recognize me from my show on the TV. I've got a lot of my fans outside and I want to miss them. Is there a way out the back?'

'Yes, sir,' he said. 'Follow me.'

He took me to the rear of the hotel and I walked off.

I went around the block in time to see all of the firm getting in taxis on their way to the station with a very heavy escort of the Old Bill. They had been asked to get the next train to London. It was just another experience to the twins; they had a laugh and went on their way.

I spent a lot of time visiting old friends in different parts of the country and invariably Chris Lambrianou would accompany me. He was a big guy, about six foot and weighing about seventeen stone. He was fun to be with and had similar aims in life to myself. I don't think he set out to be a gangster, he just wanted to make a bit of money and enjoy life without too many hiccups. He could look after himself but he wasn't interested in getting into any bother. I think if he could have got through the rest of his life without falling out with anyone he would have been happy.

I would often go to Liverpool to look up Billy Grimwood who was an old mate from prison. He was making a few bob from the legalite tables, the only form of roulette that was legal in those days. Chris's brother Tony would join us on the odd occasion. I think he had illusions of becoming a gangster even in those days.

By 1965 I had got rid of the Brown Derby club but still had a share in a casino in Mayfair. I had plenty of time on my hands and was making a few quid without having to show my face. So I decided to give my friends a visit, stuck a few grand in my pocket and arrived in Blackpool intending to stay for a week or so. But the visit lasted a lot longer than I had planned. I met a girl who was appearing at the theatre in St Anne's and we got pretty involved. Things seemed to be going right for once and I was enjoying life in general.

CHAPTER FOURTEEN

The Richardsons

I might have known things were going too smoothly. It was while I was part of the Krays' circle that I was nearly killed by the Richardsons, a rival firm, although the seeds of our disagreement had been sown before I became friendly with the twins.

As far as my association with the Krays is concerned, I was their friend for many years but I was never on the payroll. I earned my own money and I was always capable of fighting my own battles. It has never been my game to run to anyone for help if I come unstuck. Now let me explore the beginning of my rows with the Richardsons.

The Richardson brothers, Eddie and Charlie, had gained a reputation as heavy people through taking a lot of liberties with people on the fringes of the underworld. They were the proprietors of a scrapyard in south London, Peckford Metals, and were in a position to buy stuff from the lower end of the criminal fraternity. The only trouble was that they wouldn't pay the going rate and if anyone complained that he had been duped the Richardsons would see that he was beaten up for his pains. As time went on and they got wealthier – they actually owned a mine in South Africa which added to their riches – they started to torture people for a variety of reasons but all aimed at making themselves wealthier and more powerful and feared by the average criminal. They surrounded themselves with psychopaths and started a reign of terror that lasted a few years, until they were arrested and charged in the infamous Torture Trial case during the late sixties. Charlie was sentenced to twenty-five years in prison and Eddie got fifteen.

My first run in with the Richardsons took place in south London. My friend Jack Rosa asked me to come for a drink with him to the Mason's Arms in East Lane. We had been drinking in a West End club all afternoon and Jack was a little the worse for wear. I decided to stick with soft drinks in case Jack needed looking after – in my 'minder' role. I tried, unsuccessfully, to talk Jack out of going to south London as I knew he had the hump with a few people from there, in particular a guy called Jimmy Brindle. Some members of the Brindle family were pretty notorious. Jimmy was married to the sister of Frank Fraser who was also a notorious guy. In fact Fraser had a similar life to my own up until his involvement with the Richardsons. He was sentenced to fifteen years after an affray at a club in south London where one man was gunned down and many others were injured. Fraser was later sentenced to another five years over an uprising in Parkhurst Prison. He had earned a certain amount of respect from the majority of cons for his battles against prison brutality and like me was transferred around the country many times. Jimmy Brindle wasn't in Frank's class and it was only the fact that he was married to Frank's sister that made him think he could tangle with the likes of Jack Rosa.

As soon as we arrived at the Mason's Arms I felt that the atmosphere was a bit heavy, to put it mildly. But Jack was determined to have a go at Jimmy Brindle. I could also see that there were several guys with their heads together, obviously contemplating what to do in the event of the situation going further than just words. I had just managed to get Jack to leave it till another day, when he was more sober, and we were about to go through the door when out of the corner of my eye I saw Brindle, making for Jack. I pushed Jack out on to the pavement and flattened Brindle on the doorstep. Another guy tried to take a swing at me so I immediately dropped him. As I tried to get Jack into our car I saw Brindle getting up from the floor. I then gave him a good belting and left him in a heap on the pavement.

It was when I saw that another of the gang, who had just climbed out of a wagon, had something in his hand, that I realized the situation was about to get a bit heavy. I jumped into our car and drove away.

'Let's go back and give them some more,' Jack muttered.

I would have been quite happy to go back to West London and have a few drinks but Jack insisted on going to the Reform club which was just around the corner from the pub we had just left. `

We had only been in the club about twenty minutes when there was a hush and a regular who was standing at the bar said, 'Hold up! Here come the Richardsons and they're tooled up.' I looked up and saw about half a dozen men bearing down on Jack and myself. The only one I recognized was the guy I had left on the pavement shortly before. They immediately started to hit out at us with iron bars. We fought back and although Jack and I had a couple of wounds we gave as good as we got. The Richardsons eventually fled, leaving Jack and myself grinning at each other. I had the lobe of my left ear hanging off and a couple of gashes on my head. Jack looked as if he had been through a mincing machine.

We went back to my flat in Kensington and cleaned up. We then tooled up and drove to the scrapyard in south London where Jack said the Richardsons had their head-quarters. It was deserted. Then a guy stopped in a taxi and, as the cab pulled away, Jack said, 'He'll know where they are.'

I don't think the guy wanted to co-operate, he only seemed interested in depositing the booze he had consumed into the gutter. We left and went back home.

Then we started to do some homework with the intention of making a come back. Before we could take any action the police swooped on us for a series of robberies for which I received seven years. It was whilst I was doing the seven years that Reggie Kray arrived at Wandsworth. On the exercise yard Reggie said to me, 'I hear you put Brindle into hospital.' I nodded and he said, 'His brother-in-law has just arrived in the nick for his accumulated visits. So be on your guard.'

I saw Frank Fraser a couple of days later in the bath house but it was just a glaring situation and nothing came of it. I was allocated to Dartmoor and shortly afterwards, about a month later, Fraser arrived. He had a few of his pals with him but I was never very concerned. I knew that in the nick things are pretty even. I also knew that there was not one of them I would have any trouble with if it came to a man to man situation. In fact I had one or two guys who approached me in the 'Moor and said, 'If it goes off we're with you.'

But I got involved with one of my battles with authority

shortly after arriving in Dartmoor and found myself in the prison hospital. Fraser, who was working on the bin party, arrived at the hospital and said to me, through the cell door, 'Eric, people like you and me shouldn't be falling out. We've got one common enemy so let's call it a day and be friends.' This was certainly all right as far as I was concerned.

A short while later, following the murder in the chapel, I was transferred to Liverpool. It was after my release, when I had settled into club life, that I again bumped into Fraser. I was having a drink in the Log Cabin club in Wardour Street when he came in with Eddie Richardson, Jimmy Brindle, Jimmy Andrews – who was later gunned down in the street and died – and about six other guys.

Fraser came over to me, held out his hand and said, 'Will you do me a favour and shake Jimmy Brindle's hand and let's all have a drink together?'

I was quite happy to agree although I was rather surprised at how friendly everyone was – even Brindle. I was still on my guard as I'd learnt over the years exactly how much you could trust the word of a gangster. Nearly every word they speak is designed to enhance their own power and if it suited their purpose to befriend you they would tell you anything. I've heard all the claptrap over the years: 'We must stick together', 'I'd die for my friends', 'You can trust me'. All phrases that roll easily off the tongue and are meaningless. But I shook Brindle's hand and we then went our different ways.

The next time I saw Fraser and Eddie Richardson was when I got into a bit of trouble with the law whilst trying to release a guy who had been arrested outside my local pub. The law turned their attentions to me and I was arrested instead. The Kray twins sent Teddy Smith to the police station with a few quid to have a talk with a top detective. I was subsequently bailed to appear at Clerkenwell Magistrates' Court the next morning on a reduced charge. After being bailed I went to my club in the West End and I met Fraser and Eddie Richardson who had heard that I had been in trouble. They immediately gave me a few quid to help with the straightening process – to prove that bygones were really bygones. So up to then I had no problems with anyone.

A few months later I was doing business with two friends of mine, involving the laundering of some money from a small African republic. We had arranged to meet the ex-finance minister of this country at the Astor club, near Berkeley Square. My two friends were Harold Cashman, known as Boot, and Johnny, who was a member of a well-known boxing family. As we entered the Astor we saw Eddie Richardson, Fraser and most of their firm entertaining a group of Scotsmen, some of the top-rated Glasgow gangsters of the day, including Jimmy Boyle who was wanted for murder and had been brought down to London to keep out of the way for a while. There were about twenty in the group, sitting around a large table in front of the stage. We all nodded to one another in recognition and were waiting to be shown to our table when one of the jocks, who was a bit drunk, said to Johnny, 'How did you get that flat nose? Did you fall off your bike when you was a kid?'

With that Johnny hooked the guy and he went down in a heap on the floor. All the people at the Richardsons' table jumped to their feet and Boot knocked the nearest guy to the ground. Then all hell broke loose. Most of the Richardson firm grabbed bottles and started to smash them on our heads. I saw someone stab Boot. I saw Johnny run out of the fire door at the rear of the club and bent to lift Boot from the floor. I felt a knife being stuck in my head but it wasn't a serious wound and I knocked down the guy responsible. Then I heard someone shout, 'The Old Bill's arrived.'

Everyone seemed to disperse in a flash. I looked at Boot lying on the floor. He was in a bad way and I was determined to go after the Richardsons and give at least one of them the same treatment. So, without thinking of the consequences, I followed the mob up to the club entrance.

A few of them were standing around outside while one solitary policeman in uniform made his way into the club.

I saw a car pull up with Eddie Richardson driving it and I said to Fraser, 'Do you or any of your mates fancy getting into a car with me? Let's see how good you really are.'

The sweet-talking Fraser said, 'Come on, let's go somewhere else before we get nicked.'

I was willing to go with any two of them for a fight, man to man, and when Fraser told me to get in the car I thought he was accepting the challenge.

But as soon as I got in about five of them dived in after me, pulling out weapons. They were all stabbing at me with knives while I tried to get out of the car. It seemed that within minutes we were pulling up in a side street off Tottenham Court Road. As the car stopped I put one of them down and had broken out of their clutches. I almost escaped but the guy on the floor held on to the bottom of my trousers and this gave them the chance to regroup.

I could hear a few more cars pulling up and the next thing I knew I was being dragged into a basement – a workshop for one-armed bandits. I had a shotgun stuck against my head and dimly heard voices urging someone to pull the trigger. Someone else was whacking me with an axe. I heard one of them say, 'Cut his hands off. He won't be able to fight again.'

I saw the axe coming down once and put my hand up to shield my head. The blow pinned my hand to my skull. It was then I realized that I had serious injuries as I couldn't speak or move parts of my body. I must have lapsed into unconsciousness. I have only vague memories of being in a car but I recall someone saying, 'I know where to dump him.'

The next thing I remember was waking up in hospital. I still couldn't pronounce my words but I could hear people, as if at a distance, telling me I was lucky to be alive. Apparently I had been dumped on a piece of waste land and a drunken wino had stumbled across me, thinking I was a sack of rubbish. When I groaned it had nearly scared the life out of him. However he called for help and I was taken to hospital in the Holloway Road. I had over thirty serious injuries, three fractures to my skull and over three hundred stitches in various parts of my body. The only visitors I can remember were Ronnie Knight and my girlfriend Brenda. The first my family knew about it was when they read of a 'gangland attack in Mayfair'. They were a little frightened and couldn't understand the kind of life I was obviously leading.

I was ill for some considerable time but when I came out of hospital I saw the Kray twins at Vallance Road. They asked me what I felt like doing about it. I appreciated their offer of support but I had already realized that any retaliation would have triggered a major gang war possibly resulting in loss of lives. Therefore I had decided to deal with it in my own way, doing the same to the Richardsons as they had done to me. Jimmy Humphries and Jack the Hat came to see me with offers of help in case I needed it. I wanted revenge but I was still suffering physically and mentally from the attack on me and knew I didn't have a chance on my own.

One night Jack and I were following a couple of guys who had been at the Astor club with the Richardsons when we were involved in a car accident and I ended up going through the windscreen. Jack, visiting me in hospital, said, 'I don't think you're having much luck this year. Perhaps next year will be a better one for you.'

It certainly was a better one than he had.

I stayed at Jimmy Humphries' farm for a while to recuperate. Whilst there my friends Boot and Johnny came to visit me and we planned an ambush in south London. We sat outside a block of flats expecting four of the opposition to arrive. The weather was atrocious and we ended up underneath a lorry in order to keep dry. We were there until the crack of dawn but the firm never arrived and we found out later that they had gone to a party at another house.

I was carrying a gun on this and another occasion when I thought I could trap a couple of the firm. I think if I had been able to corner them I would have shot them. I've often reflected on this period of my life and been glad the way things worked out. Nothing seemed to go right for me while I was planning my revenge; it seemed as if the Richardsons had a charmed life. And I was risking a long prison sentence for carrying a gun, which was alien to me anyway.

In fact Johnny, Boot and myself were turned over by the Old Bill, who were searching for guns, as it was common knowledge that we were running around London together looking for the Richardsons. Johnny had a very lucky escape. He heard the Old Bill outside his house and stuck his gun into a shopping bag. John's wife walked to the door as if she was going shopping and was surprised to find the Old Bill outside and just about to knock.

She shouted back, 'There's some old friends at the door. I'm going to the shops.'

The Old Bill charged right past her as she calmly went off down the road.

A little while after this I heard that the Richardson firm had gone to Southport. They were nicked on their return for torturing some people and some of the firm got done for the Mr Smith's club shooting and affray. A few people were shot and one died and there were some pretty badly wounded. They were sentenced to terms of imprisonment ranging from fifteen to twenty-five years.

A lot of the minions who made up the firm were now left to their own devices. One day I was lucky to bump into one of these in a club in Bayswater. He had been boasting that his firm had done Eric Mason when I locked the door and introduced myself. I then told him that he would have to prove to all the people present how he had destroyed me, using his own words. I then gave him a humiliating time, a clout and unlocked the door to watch him scurry away.

I had another run in with a guy who liked to boast about being a member of that firm. I was walking in Gerrard Street, in Chinatown, when I recognized a man standing in the doorway of a Chinese restaurant. I immediately set about him and he squealed like a pig being slaughtered. But although satisfying, actions like this were not earning me a living so I had to get back to the graft.

The only other time I've set eyes on any other member of that firm was when I was attending a boxing event in Manchester. My friend John Shearer came over to me and told me he had just bumped into John McVicar at the bar. John Shearer had said that he was with me and John McVicar had said he would join us. Upon hearing my name another guy with McVicar had said, 'Come on, it's time to go.'

A short while later I was talking with a friend, Jimmy the Weed, when he told me that the other guy with McVicar was Eddie Richardson and apparently they were all going to a party at the Film Exchange. So I thought I would go along as I hadn't seen John McVicar for about twenty years and Eddie Richardson for even longer. We never met as they didn't go to the party.

I was to see Eddie Richardson once more after that. I had been to the Frank Bruno and Joe Bugner fight and afterwards walked into a club in Mayfair. Richardson was there with several friends. Upon seeing me he immediately said he was going to the toilet and left the club. It seems he likes to watch boxing but doesn't fancy taking part.

At the time that I was recovering from my near fatal clash with the Richardsons Ronnie was responsible for one of the most sinister moments of my life. One night I was driving home having picked up Brenda, the girl from the Pigalle show, who I was living with, when I heard on the car radio that a man had been shot in the Mile End Road. Brenda immediately said to me, 'That's where you take me for a drink sometimes. I wonder if that's anything to do with your friends?'

I didn't say anything as I had been drinking in the Grave Maurice, with the twins, earlier in the evening. When I had left to pick up Brenda everything had appeared to be quite normal.

When we got to the flat and were preparing to go to bed I switched on the radio to catch the late news. The broadcast mentioned the Blind Beggar pub and I immediately knew that it must have had something to do with the twins as nothing happened in that area without them being aware of it.

It was no surprise to me therefore when the phone rang shortly afterwards. It was Reggie. He said to me, 'Do you remember the flat over the shops in Walthamstow?'

'Yes,' I replied.

It was a well-known fact that the flat had been used before to keep people out of the way. Reggie then said, 'I want you to do me a favour. Will you go over to the flat and keep Ronnie company for a while? He'll explain everything to you.'

I turned to Brenda and said, 'I'm going out for an hour or so.'

'It's to do with that shooting isn't it?' she replied. I just smiled and left.

When I arrived at the flat I drove to the rear entrance. I could see just one light on in the kitchen and the dark sillhouette of Ronnie Kray. I climbed the stairs to the flat and knocked on the door. Ronnie came out. He seemed in a buoyant mood and said to me, 'Come in. I've got some good news for you.'

As I entered he took his jacket off and loosened his tie. He poured a drink and said, 'You should have been with me tonight. I shot that fucking Cornell's head right off.'

I couldn't believe how calm he was about it. He never told me exactly why he shot Cornell but I feel that in some ways Ronnie was annoyed that Cornell, who was a friend of the Richardsons and Frankie Fraser, was adopting an attitude of bravado because they had done me – a friend of the Krays. It may have been that Ronnie was showing me how things should have been dealt with. I stayed for a while, chatting and having a few more drinks, before I made my way home.

Ronnie and Reggie were pulled in for questioning over that business but were both released for lack of evidence. A short while after this incident I was sitting in a pub, just around the corner from their house, when they were telling a guy from south London, 'We are going to hold you responsible if that bird comes around to the house and throws any more bricks through the windows.' They were referring to the fact that George Cornell's widow had been to the house in Vallance Road and had thrown bricks through the front windows shouting, 'Murderers!' and a lot of other obscenities.

'It's embarrassing having this kind of thing going on while our mum's at home,' they said.

It was after this that Brenda said to me, 'I have a feeling that something terrible is going to happen and I'd like to get away for a couple of weeks.'

I could see that the type of life I was living – which seemed quite normal to me – was having rather an adverse effect on her. I started to notice how nervous she was getting, not for any specific reason but because of the atmosphere surrounding the people she was mixing with. Her friends in show business knew that the guy she was living with, though a night-club owner, was connected in some way with some pretty heavy people. In those days the Krays were establishing themselves and I was quite willing to help as they had been good to me. I don't think any of us saw ourselves as bad people – it was just a way of life.

For instance, one evening Reggie and I were in a club in north London when some people made some remarks and looked menacing. Reggie said to me, 'I think we've got a slight problem. I'm going to do this guy – you cop for the other one.' It was all over in a few moments but the word spread like wildfire. It was situations like this that added to the mystique of the Krays.

It was obvious to Brenda that things like this were going on. She'd overhear one-sided conversations on the telephone and she'd see the men go into a huddle away from the girls when we were discussing, for example, what to do in the event of a come-back after a member of a rival firm got hurt. It all seemed more sinister than it was. She'd see the comings and goings of men who may have looked heavy to her, although they were often just inviting the Krays to some social or sporting event. Quite a lot of these people would adopt the dress and air of the gangsters they'd seen on the screen but they were just acting a part, proving to their friends that they were friends of the mob.

Brenda never really got used to this way of life. When I first met her she was an extremely attractive woman, full of life and very bubbly, and she worked very hard. One day she would be off to Southampton to do a show for STV, the next it would be a modelling assignment. She was doing a pantomime with Norman Wisdom at Golders Green and then she started to work at the Embassy club in the show with Davy Kaye. On the odd times that we would be together she'd complain that instead of relaxing we were always out meeting my friends, that the phone would go and we'd be off to another meeting. She said, 'It's making me scared.'

I could see that she needed a rest so I suggested we went on holiday.

'I don't want a holiday but I would like to go to see my family in Leeds,' she said.

This seemed a good idea to me so we packed a few things and drove to Leeds. We went straight to Roundhay where Brenda's mum lived. I dropped her off there and went to book into the Queens Hotel. We didn't want her mum to think badly of her boyfriend and things were still pretty straitlaced in those days.

The visit worked wonders for Brenda. Within a couple of days she was her old bubbly self again. I would pick the family up and take them to lunch and meet all their friends. I was introduced as a businessman from London and I could see that Brenda's family were very proud of her.

At that time Leeds, like most cities, had one or two good nightclubs and because of the lax gambling laws most clubs would have a few gaming tables. The revenue from the tables would enable the clubs to afford the best cabaret entertainers. I decided to take Brenda and her family to the Cabaret club in North Street on the night before we went back to London. To make sure that we had a nice time I thought I would introduce myself the day before. The general manager there turned out to be Eugene Lacy, and the last time I'd seen him was in Dartmoor where he was doing twelve years. We were both surprised to be meeting under such different circumstances.

Eugene introduced me to his right-hand man, Frank Kurylo, who was to become a long-standing friend. Frank told the staff that I was a friend of the governor and to see that my company had a memorable evening. I can honestly say that I still remember that night as one of my best. Brenda was overjoyed as she was introduced from the stage as a local girl who had done well in London.

Frank went on to become Danny la Rue's personal minder and ended up something of a personality himself. If I'm in Leeds I pop into the Bridge Inn where the landlord, Ray Jessop, is a friend of mine, and give Frank a ring. He comes to see me and we talk about the old days. Thirty years later they seem like a different world.

After the Richardson gang had gone to prison, following

their convictions for torturing their victims, I decided I needed to forget about them and look to the future. I was getting a fair living but the only trouble was that I was doing too much travelling. One week I would be in London, then Nottingham or a period in Manchester and Liverpool. It was like a fast train going nowhere. I was enjoying the journey but I couldn't get off.

I realized that I had become dissatisfied with life in general. I had good days but that is all it was – a day here and a day there. I had thousands of pounds go through my hands yet I didn't own any property, had no insurance or investments. I felt that one day I was going to end up old and friendless, with nowhere to go except prison. I could see myself becoming one of the many men I'd observed over the years stumbling around the exercise yard 'bumming' for a bit of tobacco. I was finding it hard to carry on living a life that had no purpose.

It was about this time that I met George Downing in a club in Manchester, and my life took a different direction for a couple of years.

CHAPTER SIXTEEN

Betting Coups, Card Sharks and Casinos

George was one of the most flamboyant characters I ever met. When I first knew him he owned three casinos in Liverpool and had a string of race horses. He had a beautiful house near Southport, a Rolls-Royce, a lovely wife and family. A few years ago I met him in Manchester and he was very ill. He had fallen on to hard times but he still had his happy-go-lucky attitude. He was a good friend and it was a privilege to know him.

He asked me to come to work with him almost as soon as we'd met. The first thing we did was pull off a coup with one of his horses, a dead cert he'd been holding back for the right race. George used to manage a few entertainers and he had a showband appearing at a club in the north-east. So we took a few thousand pounds to Newcastle and met the road manager, a nice guy called Dave who I still see now and again at the races. George left the money with Dave together with instructions to organize the boys from the band to go to a different town each on the day of the race and find as many betting shops as they could. When we were ready we would instruct them on how to go about putting the money on the horse.

A couple of days later George and I went back to his

house, near Southport, having already dropped money off in the Midlands and London and been to see the trainer of the horse. We were now ready. We arrived back at George's house at about 7 a.m. on the day of the race and the phone soon started ringing. The boys were told to put the money on the horse in bets of no more than fifty pounds each. I then drove to Birkenhead, went to a taxi firm and asked if any of the drivers backed horses. They all pointed to one guy.

I said, 'I want you to drive me to as many betting shops as you can. I'll pay your fare and give you £10 for yourself and you can have a tenner on a cert winner.'

I was lucky – my man knew every betting shop in Birkenhead. As I came back to the car and wrote the address on each slip the driver could hardly contain himself.

'What's the horse, guv?' he asked eagerly.

I said, 'Don't worry, you'll be in on it a couple of minutes before the off.'

When we got to the last betting shop I took the driver in with me and, just before the off, told him the name of the horse. He looked it up in the paper and said, 'This hasn't got a chance. It's never been placed in about ten runs.'

'Don't worry, write your bet out. It's going to win today,' I said confidently.

Reluctantly he put his tenner on our horse. His face was a picture when the horse took up the running in the last furlong and kept on to win by a distance.

I did twenty-three betting shops in Birkenhead and in total we covered over 1,030. It took three days before we got all the money in from around the country. George and I then drove us to London where we booked into the Hilton Hotel and met the trainer and jockey to give them their cut.

Then I went to bed as I hadn't had a sleep for about five days. But not George, he went straight off to Crockfords to play a couple of shoes at chemin-de-fer.

After this episode my lifestyle changed. Every day it would be racing or casinos and lots of travelling. Being a gambler was as glamorous as my previous way of life but there was none of the violence I had come to accept as normal. I was happy making lots of money and meeting many interesting people.

Because I had organized the Joe Louis event in Manchester some friends of mine asked if I thought they could make a few quid by taking Billy Conn on a tour of personal appearances in the north of England. Billy Conn was the ex-light-heavyweight champion of the world who had come nearer than anyone to beating Joe Louis when Louis was the world champion. I thought it would be a good draw if he appeared in George Downing's casinos in Liverpool. So we did a deal and I took Billy Conn to Liverpool and arranged to meet the press at the Press club. But just before we went to the Press club I took Billy to Tommy McArdle's Victoria club as a special favour to Tommy, who was one of the great characters of Liverpool club life and also loved his boxing. We had a great couple of weeks whilst Billy Conn was in Lancashire. We took him to Haydock Park races where we opened a couple of bottles of champagne with Sir Matt Busby. We stayed at George's house for a couple of weeks and Billy said it was the best couple of weeks he'd had in many years. We certainly enjoyed his company.

At this time we became very friendly with another guy who had a couple of casinos in the East Midlands. Dudley Grace is still one of my best friends, and he and George were similar in many ways and great to be with. All three of us went to Miami with a gambling junket (a cut-price holiday arranged for casino members to visit another club abroad) and met Dino Cellini, who was the casino boss. Dudley introduced George to Dino and from then on George was in the casino morning, noon and night, giving all of the croupiers heart attacks with his fearless gambling. When Dino was in London, George and I had dinner with him in the Colony club. George, who had been losing pretty heavily, borrowed a few thousand pounds on Dino's signature. Quite a few weeks went by before Dino said to me, 'Have you seen George lately?'

I knew what he meant, so I mentioned to George that he should take a trip to London and settle with Dino.

George said, 'Don't worry about it, I'll give him a ring in a day or two.'

But about a week or so later George phoned me to ask, 'Eric, will you go and sort that problem out at the Colony? I've had a visitor to my house and he said some very sinister things about paying debts.'

I went to see Dino and sorted things out, and Dino was quite unruffled by the situation. He said, 'Unfortunately, Eric, these things have to be sorted out like this. Everyone must understand that they can't ignore a debt. Tell George to come and have some dinner and we'll all be friends.' That was the end of the matter.

I was now spending a lot of time with Dudley Grace. We'd meet at one of his casinos in Nottingham or Derby and arrange to go racing the next day. One particularly memorable week started at the Cheltenham Festival meeting, which, in my opinion, is the greatest meeting in the country. Dudley and I had taken along about £3,000 each, which twenty-five years ago was a fair lump of dough. After the first day of the three-day meeting we hadn't backed a single winner, but Dudley said to me, 'Don't worry, there's a good poker game at the 21 club this evening.' So we went to our hotel to get changed and have a bite to eat. Then after a bit of socializing in the hotel bar we went over to the 21 club where there was a very big game in progress.

Knowing Dudley's prowess with the cards I had sat back to await the inevitable outcome when I realized that things weren't going according to plan and Dudley finally got pulled into a big pot. We were left without a shilling between us and we still had the hotel bill to pay. We tramped back to the hotel, had a few drinks then bumped into a pal of ours, Billy Foulkes from Sheffield. We didn't have to tell him the story, Billy had been through it all himself on many occasions, so he loaned us a couple of hundred quid.

We went back to the track, where we bumped into a Catholic priest at the bar and he started to tell me about this horse owned by a friend of his in Ireland. Dudley was smiling and getting the drinks set up and I wandered out to look at the price of the priest's friend's horse; it was 10-1. I stuck £100 on it and went back to the bar to tell Dudley what I'd done. He nearly had a fit and said, 'I was going to have the lot on the favourite, it can't be beaten.'

With a certain amount of trepidation we went out to watch the race. It wasn't many minutes later that we were shouting the priest's friend's horse up the hill on the way to the winning post. We kept the priest with us for the next twenty-four hours and we backed about another four winners. On the third day the priest was still drunk when he flew back to Ireland and Dudley and myself went on our way.

Next stop was Long Eaton dog track where we knew that we would be given a bit of useful information – and there was always a big poker game after the dogs had finished. We got a few quid at Long Eaton then had a day's rest.

Then Dudley told me of a coup that was being set up in Leicester which was about to be put into motion. It was a rather clever but simple plot. There was a guy who was an expert at picking locks and he'd already got into the Ambassadors club in Leicester while it was closed. He then opened the cupboard where the casino kept the 'kem' playing cards. He substituted his own marked cards for the dozen packs the casino had. All that he had to do then was to sit in with an accomplice and it wouldn't be long before all the money came their way. Within a few days we had cleaned up and won thousands of pounds.

Dudley and myself had quite a lot of strange experiences in the gambling world. One of the most memorable periods of my life started with what I at first thought was a coincidence – I was later to find out it was no such thing.

Dudley and I were having a night out at the Talk of the Town, in London, when a guy lumbered past our table knocking over a bottle of champagne. I immediately jumped up to remonstrate with him, whereupon he became very apologetic and ordered a bottle of the club's best champers for us. He was very charming and apologetic, so much so that I felt sorry for his embarrassment and invited him to join us in a drink, which he did. When he paid for the bottle we couldn't help noticing that he had a roll of money so big he could hardly pull it out of his pocket.

All we knew at this point was that his name was Joe Robino and he was from the States. He was one of the biggest men I've ever met, weighing about twenty-five stone. With his big smiling face he seemed quite harmless. We naturally drifted into conversation about what he did for a living and very shortly we were being invited to Joe's room at the Hilton for a drink and a game of cards.

In London there is a very popular game called rummy (outside London they call it London rummy). Anyway, Big Joe said it was rather like a game he had played with his mum back home when he was a kid. We fell for it hook, line and sinker and over the next couple of hours he cleaned Dudley and I right out. We were absolutely dumbstruck and had to have a drink and some sandwiches to recover while Joe went for a shower.

He left all of the money he'd won on the shelf of an open wardrobe. When he came out of the shower I saw him glance towards the cash, then he sat down and said, 'Take your money back, you had no chance of winning with me.' He told us what his plan had been from the very first time he'd joined us in the Talk of the Town. He wanted to meet someone who knew all the ropes about the private games in London, or anywhere else for that matter. Just for introducing him and looking after him we would be on 40 per cent of all his winnings. Dudley didn't fancy it and he had his business to think of but I decided to give it a go.

The first club I took Joe to was the 45 club in Cromwell Road. It was quite normal for me to go there as I used the place regularly and I also had a business interest in the place. It was ideal as Joe told me he didn't care if there were hustlers or professionals there, he could handle them. Most of the gambling clubs in Earl's Court and Kensington were full of grafters looking for easy pickings but by now I sat on the same side of the table as Joe so I thought I would be able to spot something. I also took all the side bets, so I had a very big interest in what he was winning.

I watched Joe very carefully when he played and I couldn't believe my eyes. I saw him pick up his hand, and to use a gambler's expression he would have a handful of dolly mixtures. Then after two or three dips at the pack, his hand would be pat and he'd call up. It was uncanny. I watched him operate hundreds of times in various clubs throughout Britain and I never ever saw what he did. I made thousands of pounds with Joe.

I was in the Colony club one night having dinner with George Raft and Dino Cellini when I asked them if they knew Joe.

Dino said, 'Eric, whatever you do, don't play with him or he'll skin you alive. He's the best, and his photo is in every casino in the States. That's why he's over here.'

I didn't say any more but when I saw Joe I told him what I'd heard and he just laughed.

He said, 'Don't worry about them, you'll get a better living with me and certainly more laughs.' He was right about that.

The last time I saw Joe was as I was going into the Mount club in Mayfair. There was an Australian guy telling Joe that the place was closed; we couldn't understand it as it was always open. Joe and I went for a drink and I saw the Aussie later that night and he said to me, 'I'm sorry I couldn't say anything about what happened earlier on, as I didn't know who the big guy was, but Scotch Jack Buggy was shot in there earlier on and they were still getting rid of the body.'

I took the story with a pinch of salt at first then I read a while later that Scotch Jack's body had been found, rolled in a carpet, by two off-duty policemen fishing in the sea.

I was also acting as minder to some of the Arabs coming over to London with money to burn. They all loved to gamble and never seemed to go to bed. A friend of mine made his living by organizing parties and trips to casinos and nightclubs for clients who were mainly Arabs. He would ring me and say 'There's this prince' – they were all princes or sheiks – 'who wants to go to a few clubs and speilers and he also wants to go to the Derby. Would you look after him?' I'd agree and then meet my friend later at the Stork club where I'd be paid. I could earn £500 on a good day. I met some great guys from the Middle East, including the son of the Jordanian ambassador who was to be a good friend for quite some time. He was also a very good card player.

It was around this time that I started to hear rumours that Jack the Hat had been murdered and that he had died a pretty horrific death. It was also said that he had been lured to his death by some people that were supposed to be his friends, as well as mine. Gradually the story began to take shape, and it seems that the Lambrianou brothers had made sure Jack had enough drink inside him to be incapable of defending himself. That, to me, is a cold, calculating, heartless way to treat someone who was supposed to have once been your friend.

I couldn't help thinking of the time I was nearly hacked to death in the basement off Tottenham Court Road – Jack must have felt much as I did when Reggie Kray stabbed him to death. There was a difference though – my row was a gang fight brought about by a clash of personalities; Jack was completely unaware of the fate that was waiting for him when he was drinking at the bar of the Regency club with people slapping him on the back and telling him what a great guy he was. And then when he was nearly incapable, saying 'Let's go to the Kray twins' party.'

I often think of all the times that I had with Jack. I couldn't have had a better mate and I can relate a score of incidents that prove Jack was a different person to the out of control gangster I've read about lately. I've spoken quite recently to people who knew Jack as well as I did, and most say he was the type of guy I've described. Admittedly, there are others who say, 'Eric, you didn't know him a couple of years before he died – he'd changed.'

Jack must have changed a fair bit but I can't imagine him deserving the kind of death that befell him. One of the saddest moments of my life came when I met Anne, Jack's ex-wife, at a party. She asked me if I knew exactly what had happened to Jack. I told her what I had heard and she said, 'Jack never deserved that kind of death. He was a good man, he never meant any harm to anyone.' I was completely choked up.

I like to remember Jack as the chap who stuck with me through some pretty grim times, someone you could always rely on. I'm sure I'm not the only person who remembers Jack with a lot of affection – he was a brave, tough, fun-loving guy.

I was also beginning to hear rumours about the disappearance of Frank Mitchell, who had apparently been gunned down after he had been sprung from Dartmoor. But though the rumour was very strong, no one seemed to know who had actually killed Frank. The Krays were blamed but I have always been convinced that it was nothing to do with them. They both thought the world of Frank and there was absolutely no reason for them to do it.

Apart from the sadness about losing two friends, I was otherwise enjoying life. I spent quite a lot of time commuting between London, Nottingham and Liverpool. I'd sometimes pop in to see old mates when I was visiting London and sometimes there would be a bit of lucrative work. It was at one of these particular jaunts that I renewed my acquaintance with John McVicar.

CHAPTER SEVENTEEN

John McVicar and the Aussie Shoplifters

I first met John McVicar when I was the owner of the Emerald Beach club in Soho. John was in his early twenties and he started to frequent the West End in company with his sister Janice and a few of her girlfriends. He was always very quiet and polite and seemed out of place with most of the clientele of the club, as they were mainly guys who had acquired a few quid and wanted everyone to see that they had been successful – notwithstanding which quite a lot of them would be skint within a few weeks. John always seemed to have a few notes to spend but didn't talk much about what he did. His sister was a bubbly type of girl, well liked by everyone, and it was always nice to see them in the club.

I then took over the Brown Derby club which was frequented by much the same clientele. I saw John a few times and then heard that he was in trouble and had received a fairly long sentence for armed robbery. As the years pass you hear or read things in the newspapers about people that you've met and so it was with John. I read that he and some other cons had overpowered the screws on their way from one prison to another and eventually had their sentences extended to over twenty years.

A few years later I had given up the club business and had gone back to crime myself. It's a funny life, you come out of prison hoping to go straight, build up a business, work sixteen hours a day and as soon as you get on your feet you have the law harassing you for every trivial thing they can think of, until you are forced out of business and back into crime. They'd come to the club at all times, checking that all the customers were members or *bona fide* signed-in guests of a particular member, checking a genuine meal was supplied for the supper licence extension. It was impossible to stick to the letter of the law and be successful as people wouldn't come to the club if they were being hassled all of the time. I couldn't hold a licence with my criminal record so I had to find someone else to be the licence holder. Of course, when the club was charged with some infringement it was the licensee who was fined and as a result licensees were hard to come by. In the end I was forced out of the business and ended up doing the same as most of my ex-customers – executing a robbery and going to the various clubs to spend the proceeds.

It was a few days after a particular robbery when I read the papers and saw that there had been a daring escape from Durham Prison. One of the people who had escaped was John McVicar together with Walter Probyn, my old friend from the Wandsworth days. Alas, poor old Walter had broken his leg in their dramatic bid for freedom.

I, like most people, followed the story for the next forty-eight hours, whilst the press made John public enemy No. 1 and said he was surrounded and couldn't get away from the north of England. I then went on my usual rounds, ending up in a club called Oscars in Albermarle Street, Mayfair. As soon as I walked in, a friend came over and said, 'I've been phoning around for you. There's someone here to see you.'

I thought I was dreaming – there stood John McVicar at the end of the bar. Every policeman in Britain must have been thinking what a feather in his cap it would be if he could nick John, and there he was calmly drinking a soft drink in one of the most popular clubs in London.

I was working with a little team from north London at the time and one of them was from a well-known boxing family. No one would think of his house so I took John there straight away. John, myself and a couple of pals sat around half the night chatting and generally working out John's immediate plans. He was safe where he was for a couple of days but then he needed to get together with his missus and little boy. We organized a few quid, clothes and a car, and with his missus got them a flat in south London.

I saw John a few times after that. There were a few hairy incidents at the time and we nearly walked into an ambush once. John was to meet me and another guy in Stoke Newington. He arrived at the meet early and decided to go into a betting shop near by. Quite by chance there was a policeman inside who had been involved with John on a case before he went inside. Luckily John recognized the policeman at the same time as the policeman recognized him. As we arrived we saw the Old Bill charging up mob-handed. If John had not spotted the policeman, and he had followed John, we'd have walked into a trap.

John, meanwhile, sprinted off and being a pretty fit guy

he soon disappeared from view. Discreetly leaving the scene ourselves we saw John drive off in the car we'd found for him so we knew he was safe for the time being.

Some of the people that I worked with in those days were like me and enjoyed travelling. We would spend quite a lot of time on the Continent, mainly in France, Italy and Switzerland. It was amazing how quickly we would find who the local villains were. I think it is because all villains like the night life, no matter what country they are from, and once you are noticed spending plenty of money in the clubs the locals soon cotton on. So it wasn't long before we were meeting people in Shalako's in Brussels, the Red House in Zurich, or the Lucky Strip in Paris and swapping tales with each other. One guy we met in Paris was an old retired villain named Jacques. He had a hotel in Paris and another home in Vichy. Jacques was to become a very useful connection for me especially when I was travelling around the continent with the shoplifting gang.

In the early sixties, just before I was released from prison, I used to manage to get hold of the odd newspaper, even though I would probably be in the punishment block. One day I read an article entitled 'The Australian Shoplifting Gang'. What made it interesting to me was that a guy, who had been mentioned in the article and had been arrested with the Aussie gang, was an old friend of mine and was rated as a very smart operator among the criminal fraternity. So I thought, What is he doing mixed up with a load of petty thieves? Then it seemed that nearly every day there was an article in the press about the influx of Aussie criminals coming into this country and, far from being petty criminals, they were getting away with millions of pounds.

It wasn't long after my release from jail that I met a lot of these guys, as they moved in the same circles as myself and some of them used the Brown Derby while I was the proprietor. They were not just the ordinary shoplifters. They would walk into a jeweller's shop, very smartly dressed; invariably with a woman wearing an expensive mink coat and carrying a bouquet of flowers, all props to distract the assistants; cleverly open the showcases or the window displays and come away with thousands of pounds' worth of diamonds.

They were not only into shoplifting, but were some of the smartest con-artists I have ever met and done business with. It was the type of thing that now appealed to me, along with gambling, as no one ever got hurt and there were some pretty rich pickings and relatively light punishment if you were caught, plus the opportunity to travel to the Continent regularly.

With all of the publicity that the Australians were getting it was a lot better if they had a few people with them who didn't speak with their accent, to 'front up', whilst visiting certain well-known Bond Street jeweller's. I was to spend a couple of years with our Commonwealth cousins and I made a lot more money with those people than I did as a bank robber.

The first Australian I was to do any business with was a guy with a similar background to my own. He had done fifteen years in Australia and was a known tough guy. He had realized there were people making a fair living who were only risking a few months in prison if they got caught. His name was Keith and he, like a lot of the Aussies, found that there was a much bigger pond to 'fish in' by getting a flight to the mother country and having an extended holiday.

I soon came to know everyone in the team. Nearly every one of them had a nickname, most self-explanatory. They were Jack the Liar, Crying Steve, Morrey the Head and Roy the Boy amongst others. There were about twenty of the original team including some very smart girls, such as Carmen, who I was to visit later in Holloway Prison when she was on remand, awaiting trial for stealing nearly £250,000 worth of jewels from the Hilton Hotel. Also Grace, an elegant lady, who one day I spent some time with getting out of a northern town with her bra stuffed with diamonds.

I was to have many escapades with my Australian friends. One of the cleverest of the team was a guy called Barry. He was a great character, always laughing and absolutely fearless. I remember at the height of all the publicity about the Australian gang the police told the press that they were to give a lecture and demonstration at a particular jeweller's on how best to combat this rising new crime wave. Barry couldn't wait for the day and he duly turned up at the jeweller's, where the police were demonstrating the best methods of preventing the criminals from stealing jewels. You can imagine the laughter from the team when the evening papers splashed the headline JEWEL THIEF STEALS EMERALD WHILST POLICE DEMONSTRATE ANTI-THEFT METHODS.

I went all over the Continent with Barry, Roy, Keith,

Danny and Grace and we had some great times. The best thing that happened to us was when we booked into a nice comfortable hotel just off the Rue Laffiette in Paris. We got into conversation with the proprietor, Jacques, and found he was an old retired villain. Within a very short time he was buying all of our gear, so we didn't then have to keep taking the risks by bringing the fruits of our labour back through the Customs at Heathrow.

We had, in Paris alone, about ten good tickles from jewellers' shops. In fact we were responsible for one of the biggest heists ever, using one of the variations on a standard method for tricking the staff. It all seemed so easy at the time. It was nothing for us to fly out of Paris in the morning, into Switzerland and back the same day, with the contents of some jeweller's window. We found that Amsterdam was a veritable Aladdin's cave. We could go to practically any street in Amsterdam and find enough work to keep us in absolute luxury.

We stayed in good hotels in all the cities we worked in. One day we'd be in the American Hotel in Amsterdam, the next it would be the FrankfurterHof in Frankfurt or the SwitzerHof in Zurich, then possibly the Grand in Stockholm, or the Palace in Milan. Then, when we'd get back to London, there would be another member of the team with a different scheme to go for.

Danny, who was like one of the Godfathers to the Australian contingent, always had somebody arriving from Oz who had a new scam or other. One of the best of these was a guy who arrived accompanied by a little chap who was a dead ringer for Ron Hutchinson, the top Australian jockey who was riding in England at that time. All they had to do was find the big punters, which was pretty easy to do if you kept your eyes and ears open at the race tracks. They would then engage the punter in conversation, arrange a series of meetings and by a strong coincidence, the Ron Hutchinson lookalike would arrive at the restaurant or bar or wherever the meeting was being held.

They would then get into deep conversation with Danny and pass over what was supposed to be inside information, for which the Hutch would be seen to receive a large packet of money, presumably for past information provided. The punter would be very impressed, especially when he was manoeuvred into going to the car park, to see the Hutch off to his car, which always had some jockey's gear lying casually on the back seat.

It was then that the hard work had to be done by finding a winner to give to the punter. Danny was a pretty good tipster anyway and by the time the punter was ready he would trust the boys implicitly. The whole art of the con game is to make the punter impatient to get on with the business, so if anything went wrong you could always say, 'You should have had more patience and then things would have gone right.' However, after a time they found that by getting a few punters, they could give two or three red-hot tips in the same race to the individuals, thereby guaranteeing a 'pay-off' to at least one very satisfied punter. This game eventually came apart when, a few years later, another jockey, George Moore, came from Australia and the same lookalike method was used. However, when a few disgruntled punters started to threaten the real George Moore at the race tracks and started to send nasty letters to his home, he, obviously being a completely innocent party to the scam, went to the police. I believe the publicity forced him to go back to Australia.

Everybody seemed to benefit from the influx of the Australians, especially the club owners and restaurant proprietors in Bayswater and Queensway, as it was normal for all of the team to meet in the various clubs that were dotted around the area. There was a favourite place in Bayswater Road called the Caravelle club. It was a regular haunt for the criminal fraternity and also for many actors and sportsmen. One actor who seemed to use the club quite regularly was Ian Hendry who was a very popular chap with the Australians. He had recently made a film called *The Hill* where he played the part of a brutal prison guard. One of the Aussies took umbrage to Ian after seeing the film and started taking him to task for being so brutal to the prisoners. Everyone soon realized that the guy who'd seen the film had got the part that Ian had played mixed up with reality and that things could get out of hand. Then Ian barked at the guy, 'Stand to attention and put that drink down when you speak to me.' The Australian, without thinking, did as he was told and everyone in the club burst out laughing. The tension was gone and Ian became one of the most popular guys in the club.

A great friend of Ian Hendry's who used to visit the club regularly was Ronald Fraser, another well-known actor, who used to relate great stories about Robert Mitchum. We would spend hours in that club drinking and telling stories. Whenever any of the girlfriends of the Oz crowd came over from Sydney or Melbourne they would get very excited and come to the various clubs and drink at the bar with actors like Ian Hendry, Ronnie Fraser and Sean Connery. He was a really charming fellow and I remember one Australian girl just couldn't believe she was standing next to the great man when he said, 'I've got to play in a golf tournament in Bognor tomorrow, so I'll have to get to bed early.'

I said to Sean, 'I'll give you a lift to your hotel.'

When I got back to the club, the Australian girl was in a state of shock and could hardly speak. It took her months to get over the fact that he was just an ordinary guy who had gone off to bed early, on his own, so as to be on time for a game of golf the next morning.

There's a lovely story that arose from the association between the acting fraternity and the Aussies. A well-known actor was about to get engaged and casually mentioned that he was looking for a nice ring for his prospective bride. The word was given out that there was a customer for a good ring. Roy the Boy just happened to be in Harrods a couple of days later and asked one of the assistants to show him some rings. With a little bit of sleight of hand he acquired a nice stone worth £5,000. He immediately brought it over to the club and sold it for £2,000. That ring would be worth well over £50,000 now, so some lucky actor made a good investment in his early days.

I believe most of the Aussie team eventually ended up back in Australia, after a tour through the United States, where they apparently got some pretty rich pickings.

After the Aussies went back home I hung around in London for a while and then went back to work with George Downing. We would travel about quite a lot; Manchester, Liverpool and Southport, always using the various casinos to pick up a few bob. It was amazing to see the number of grafters who were all using the same clubs.

You could walk into a club in Southport and see Geordie, who every card sharp and grafter knew, then a couple of days later you could walk into another club in Birmingham and there would be the same Geordie. Or it might be Scotch Alec who happened to be Greek. I don't know where the nickname came from, but he was a remarkable chap who nearly always worked on his own. His only gimmick was a handkerchief he used to mop his brow with. He loved a drink and I've spent many hours with Alec after he'd just cleaned up on some gaming table.

The British casinos in the sixties were like manna from heaven and I think every grafter in the world came here for easy pickings. I've seen them all and seen some amusing incidents in various clubs and casinos all over the country.

I was in a casino in Manchester with George Downing and Joe Marlow when they had the croupier straightened as he was dealing seconds. To make it easier to slip the second card out, instead of the top one, he used french chalk on the cards and when he shuffled he would do the cut shuffle by running the cards crossways into each other. All of a sudden he forgot himself, rippled the cards in the normal way and a big cloud of dust went into the air.

There was a stunned silence and a punter who had been losing pretty heavily got up from the table and left the club. He was back in about twenty minutes with two parcels. He threw one on the table with a thud in front of the croupier and started to open the other. Both contained a small axe.

The fellow said calmly, 'Am I going to have my money back or are we going to duel for it?' There was no argument, the bloke got his money back and everyone went for a drink.

Malcolm Rance was a great character from Manchester who I first met years before in Dartmoor. He was a very tough guy but he'd retired from the heavy game and had learnt a bit of sleight of hand. He wasn't as good as some of the chaps I had seen but he still made a fair living. I was in a club in Wales with him one night when he was working the blackjack table with extra cards. He used to sit at the blackjack table with his legs bent up and would lodge the spare cards at the back of his bent leg. Now one of the croupiers tumbled that he was using extra cards and told security. I saw the security man go to phone the police so I tipped off Malcolm. He didn't turn a hair. He called the security bloke over and said, 'Could you organize me some drinks, and have one yourself.'

With that he handed the security bloke a tenner to give to the girl at the bar.

Unbeknown to me, or anyone else, Malcolm had put the spare cards into the security guy's pocket. When the police came and accused Malcolm he was very indignant, and said bitterly, 'This is the way they treat people just because they win.' He demanded that the police search him, which they did. Of course they didn't find anything. Everyone ended up apologizing and off we went. I would have loved to have seen the security guy's face when he found the cards.

One of the most embarrassing incidents in my life happened to me in Nottingham around this time. The British middleweight title fight between Wally Swift and Johnny Pritchard, two local boys, was being held at the ice-rink. I had an interest in a business in Nottingham so a few friends had phoned me to ask me to arrange the tickets, hotel, dinner and nightclubs. I was pleased to do this as I hadn't seen some of them for a year. In the end I booked about ten people into the Old Victoria Hotel.

Everyone arrived about midday and we all got together for lunch and a few drinks. I arranged to call at the hotel later and take everyone to the fight. After the fight we went to the Pigalle club where some ladies joined the company. Then one of the boys said, 'Eric, I hear they have a big chemin-de-fer game in this town?' I told them that it was at the Society club but it would be hard to get a place at the table. They were still keen so I said I'd see what could be done.

I took three of the guys to the Society and signed them in. The boss of the club was Polish, a very nice and affable chap, who made us all welcome. I asked him if he could fix a spot in the game for one of my friends. As soon as somebody left the table he beckoned to me that there was an empty place. However, when I told my pal that there was an empty place, he said to one of the other guys in the party, who I didn't know, 'Bill, you take the seat while I have a drink.'

I didn't think there was anything suspicious about this until I noticed how often I was hearing, *'Neuf à la banc.'* Bill was starting to amass a pretty sizeable fortune. By now everyone was surrounding the table, drawn by the phenom-enon· of a guy doing something like a twelve-timer. I watched him closely but I couldn't detect anything unto-ward, except that every time he got his cards he made a rather flamboyant gesture towards the canopied light shade.

Eventually the game broke up with nearly everyone skint apart from Bill who had all of the money. We moved back to the Old Victoria Hotel. It was only then, when Bill wanted to give me a large bundle of notes, that I was certain the game had been bent. But they denied it when I raised the matter so I had to accept what they said. I left shortly afterwards and went back to my flat.

I was to get a rude awakening in the morning with someone banging loudly on my door. When I looked through the spy-hole I saw Jon the Pole, practically foaming at the mouth. He had a large pack of cards in his hand and, when I opened the door, he tossed them all up in the air shouting, '*Neuf! Neuf! Neuf!* Where are your friends? I count twenty spare *neufs* in my box.'

After I had calmed him down, he told me that when he checked the box that all the used cards had been thrown into, he had found twenty spare nines. Eventually I was able to convince him that I had also been duped. It wasn't until a few months later that I obtained the truth. I was at Cheltenham races and bumped into my friend. He admitted to me that Bill had plotted it all before they came to Nottingham. I was also right in my supposition about him 'ringing' the cards as his hands went past the light shade. I don't know who coined the phrase 'Honour among thieves', but I've never seen much of it.

When I heard that the Kray twins had just been arrested I was saddened but not surprised. I had grown up in the criminal fraternity and had gone along with all of their clichés about themselves – 'We'll stick together', 'I'd die for you', 'We're men of principle'. In reality 'men of principle' meant 'men of money'. It didn't seem to matter how many principles a man had so long as he had money. A bloke that was spending money with the firm was a lot more important than a guy who would stick with you if you were outnumbered in a battle. I found that all of the people I had been associating with had the gang mentality. They had surrounded themselves with hangers-on who had become mixers and held a certain sway because they had plenty of ready cash and were able to settle a few personal scores. It suited them to mix it for people like Jack the Hat because he openly slagged them off as wimps and hangers-on. When I heard the rumours about what had happened to Jack I thought, So much for sticking together.

When the Krays and other members of the firm were arrested my first thought was, I'm glad I'm away from it all. I had in fact just pulled a job that had netted myself and a friend a fair bit of money and we were busy enjoying ourselves. But I gave a lot of thought to Violet Kray, the twins' mother, as everyone who met her was impressed by her devotion to her sons. She never saw any bad in them, and I knew that she would be thinking that they were being fitted up by the law. She was a wonderful woman.

Of course I followed the story in the press and through the grapevine and it began to emerge that only staunch people were sticking by the twins. I felt a kind of sadness because I had had some good times with them. I realized that because of the kind of hangers-on they had attracted they had gone down a different path to the one they had planned in the early days.

CHAPTER EIGHTEEN

First-Division Criminal

Shortly after my little forays around the British casinos, and as a result of a chance meeting in the South of France, I started to associate with some of my old 'bandit' friends. I was staying at a hotel in Nice with a couple of friends and we happened to visit the Mediterranean Casino. As soon as we walked in we saw a couple of guys I'd known for a few years who were pretty heavily into bank robbery. They assured me that this was purely a pleasure trip after a successful raid in London so we had a sociable couple of days in Nice and then moved down to San Remo on the Italian Riviera where we spent a lot of time in the casino. But it was costing too much to live in that style, so it wasn't long before we were back in London, and I was renewing acquaintances with my old mates. We quickly pulled off a couple of raids that netted some fair money but we were always on the lookout for the 'big one', the ambition of every first-division criminal.

As the years had passed by and bank raiders had got more daring so the security of the banks became more challenging; and it also became something of a challenge to beat this increased security. At first, when people started to carry out daylight raids on banks, it was usually as a blagger; that is, snatching the money from the security guards taking wages or spare cash to a feeder bank.

Although security in that area got tighter, you could still easily leap over the counter and take money from the night-safe and the tills.

Raids were frequent and those in the know could identify the different operators by their *modus operandi*. We all seemed to use the same clubs and pubs and we became rather like an exclusive social club. It would be nothing for a particular team to ask someone from another to join, if they were short-handed on a particular robbery.

When the banks started to put bandit-glass up in front of the tellers, you had to keep yourself fit to enable you to get over the top. Eventually the glass was fitted right up to the ceiling, and it became hard to find a bank in London without this type of barrier. So we started to look further afield and eventually we discovered that Cardiff had never had a bank robbery – until then. As I also knew of a safe house in that city a friend and I went there to have a look at a few banks in the city centre. The first one that interested us was a major bank. On first inspection it looked an ideal job – plenty of money to be had and a very good escape route in the event of anything going wrong. We soon realized, however, that it would take too big a team to do it successfully but we looked around and found at least half a dozen banks that would be fairly easy to do.

Finally we settled for Barclays, in Albert Road, as the getaway route was a lot better than any of the others. Also, the security van which delivered and took money from the bank always arrived on time. We had no difficulty in setting the whole thing up.

After a few weeks of observation we decided to raid the bank at 10 a.m. on a Monday. We arranged to travel to

Cardiff early on the Sunday to give us time to make sure that everything was in place for the following morning. There was a Transit van to be put away with all of our tools; there were two cars as change-over vehicles and the last check over the getaway route to be organized, to make sure there were no road blocks since we'd last been over the route. The safe house was a mile away from the city; the house of an old retired villain who could be trusted. The Transit van had been stolen a week before and the number plates had been changed to correspond to a similar van that we had taken the tax-disc from. Hence there were two identical vans that hadn't been reported missing. We did the same to two Ford Cortinas on the Saturday before the robbery. The one that we took from outside Chelsea football ground, we later discovered belonged to a police inspector.

When we arrived on the Sunday I went to my old friend's house to check that he'd rented a couple of lock-up garages. He was rather thrilled at the prospect of being involved in a bank robbery, albeit only in a non-active role. As he pointed out, he was getting a bit old for jumping over bank counters, but he'd settle for the excitement and a few quid which he could certainly do with.

One of the team had already travelled to Cardiff from Paddington Station with some ordinary looking baggage, containing two sawn-off shotguns, Balaclava helmets, gloves, valises for carrying the money, plus one or two extras that go to make up a bank-robber's working kit. The shells in the shotguns had been doctored to make them non-lethal by taking out the pellets and substituting ordinary household rice. However, they would sound just the same when fired. We were a team of experienced people who had all boxed at various levels: a couple of pro-fighters and the others could look after themselves, in any circumstances, so we didn't need shotguns as weapons. The idea was to create as much confusion as possible whilst we helped ourselves to the rewards.

We knew that on Monday at 10 a.m. there would be fourteen or fifteen night-safe pouches on the ledge behind the counter. There would be four tills open with about £3,000 in each. There would also be a large bag waiting for the security people to take to the main Barclays branch. They would also be delivering a bag of new notes. We knew from experience that it would take us only one minute after entering the bank until we left with the loot; the press referred to us as the Minute Men.

Everyone knew their job. The bandit screen was only built to a height of about six feet above the counter, so two men would immediately leap up on to the counter and then drop down inside the working area of the bank. By this time the two security men would have been overpowered by the other two members of the team. The job went according to plan, without a serious hitch; but there was always the chance that the odd incident, either scary or amusing, would occur. This particular robbery had a bit of both.

When the security van pulled up outside the bank the two security men went immediately to the hatch at the rear and, as it opened, took a large package from it. One of them carried the package into the bank while the other followed him in, brandishing a baton. It was then we struck. My job was to take care of the baton man, who would be standing just inside the door while his mate would go to a communicating door to transfer the money bags. Terry and I went through the door immediately behind them. Terry's job was to smash the glass in the door frame and fire a shot into the ceiling, thus causing maximum confusion. My job had been taken care of in the split second I'd taken to flatten the guard. The other two were already on their way over the counter.

There were four customers in the bank and I told them all to sit on the floor and nothing would happen to them. Three of them complied without a murmur but one guy, who was paying in his takings from an ice-cream firm, wanted to argue with the bank staff as to whose money it was. Quite oblivious of the danger he was in, he kept insisting that as he had already put his money on to the bank's counter, it was therefore legally in the bank now. The bank teller was begging him to do as he was told and get down. In fact, all the bank staff wanted to do, by this time, was comply with our demands and lie down behind the counter. I took the disputed bag of money from the counter and threw it into the valise with the other we had taken from the security man. Although he'd finally got to the floor with everyone else, the ice-cream man was still giving a running commentary on the legal implications as to liability for the stolen money.

The two chaps behind the counter were hurriedly filling their valise, which was soon bulging with the money from the night-safe pouches and the tills. As they came through the communicating door they picked up the bags that were waiting for the security men, plus the two that were on our side of the counter, and we were all ready to leave. As we came out of the bank a passer-by attempted to obstruct us; he was pushed aside and we leapt into the Transit van for the getaway. That chap was later rewarded for his bravery.

As we pulled away from the bank we immediately began to pack everything into the two large bags, the money into one, and all the equipment into the other. We were soon at the first change-over. I drove one of the Fords to the safe house with the money, while the other dropped the guy with the tools at the station to take the first train out, wherever it was going; eventually to make his way back to London. The cars were parked in another part of the city.

We then cut the money up into equal shares, after taking out the 'bung' for my friend. One of the boys took two shares, his own and one for the guy who had gone with the tools. He made his way back to a van, with pigeons in it, as these were his cover. He drove into the countryside, releasing the pigeons as he made his way home. We all met the next day without any hitch. After the usual shopping spree it was off to our favourite club where we analysed the previous day's work. There was the usual feeling of exhilaration and a few laughs of disbelief at the guy who was arguing about the ownership of the money whilst the robbery was in progress. Also at the bank teller, haughtily telling one of our team who had leapt over the bandit screen, that he shouldn't be this side of the counter, before she realized it was a bank raid. There was also grudging admiration for the guy who had tackled us.

Ironically, it was the takings from the ice-cream firm that allowed the police to finally build up a strong case against us. One of the team had some of this money on him when he was arrested and the cashier from the ice-cream firm recognized his scrawl on the notes when he had made the parcels of money up. A handwriting expert gave evidence to support him.

I was at the time living with a girl who I'd previously met in a club, and we had one of those old-fashioned televisions that looked like a piece of furniture with doors on the front. It also had a large space with speakers on either side, with a big gap in between. I put a few thousand pounds into the gap, screwed the back cover on and left it. It was about two weeks after the robbery in Cardiff, at about seven in the morning, when there was a knock on the door. Thinking it was a builder, who had come to do some work on the house, I told my girlfriend to tell him to come back at about 10 a.m., as it was still too early in the morning. The sound of her footsteps on the stairs was immediately followed by the heavy thump of boots. I'd heard this sound before and was just sitting up as they burst through the door. I found myself staring down the barrels of two guns.

'Move and you're dead,' said the plain-clothes inspector.

It wasn't difficult to see that I wasn't concealing a weapon as I didn't have a stitch on. They let me pull on my strides and shirt. By this time I could hear them tearing the place apart. There must have been about a dozen of them and the only place they didn't look was inside the back of the television. We were all arrested at the same time, courtesy of a little information from the brother-in-law of one of the team.

We were taken to Cardiff, charged and remanded to Cardiff Prison. We were the first Category A prisoners to go there and, after a trial before Mr Justice Bridge, we were sentenced to long terms of imprisonment. I got ten years.

CHAPTER NINETEEN

The Arab

After being sentenced for bank robbery I was sent back to Wandsworth Prison for assessment and allocation. I found that in the years since my release from my previous sentence a lot had changed inside. Following the Mountbatten Report a system of categories had been introduced and people such as myself were immediately put down as Category A. This meant that we were considered to be a danger to the public, other prisoners and to anyone who worked within the prison.

Consequently a Cat. A prisoner was locked in his cell for twenty-three hours a day and only allowed out into the prison yard to exercise, by himself, under the supervision of three or four screws. This would go on for a couple of months until he was either allocated and sent to a top security Cat. A prison or deemed by the allocation board to be considered worthy of another chance and made Cat. B. In the latter case he was still probably locked up for twenty-three hours a day but was allowed to exercise with other prisoners.

Being locked up nearly all day, I had plenty of time to reflect upon my life, both over my past and what the future had to hold for me. It was a pretty gloomy picture. This prison stretch was different to the first. I was older and I knew that if things went wrong for me I would probably never see life outside the prison walls again. I had mellowed a lot and had got used to a comfortable lifestyle and now I had the prospect of some pretty spartan times ahead.

I knew, of course, that I still had a fair lump of money hidden but I didn't think that my girlfriend was the type to wait a few years. I had visions of some other man sleeping in my bed, wearing my clothes and spending my money. I knew from experience how seldom a man's partner will wait for him once he is locked up. In fact I was lucky – she waited a few months before she did the moonlight flit. I was expecting it and when the chaplain came to my cell with a letter in his hand I was a little prepared.

He said, 'The Governor's concerned about this letter that's been sent to you and he's asked me to come to speak to you, in case there's anything we can do.'

I thought, Well at least she's taken the time to write to me. As I read the letter telling me that she had met someone else and that she had been worried about the 'stuff' in the television and burnt it, I was a little hurt but quite calm. I thanked the chaplain for his concern and asked him to thank the Governor and told him not to worry that I'd do anything silly.

Getting that letter was the real turning point for me. It brought back the futility of the life I had led, the realities of what a small world the underworld is. I met a lot of good people during my life of crime and rebellion, people I have a lot of respect for, but I also met many who had no redeeming features, who were beneath contempt. Today, when I go walking or jogging early in the morning near my home, and I pass ordinary people maybe out walking their dog, and they say, 'Good morning', I get an enormous feeling of pleasure. I realize that now I am part of the real world.

I was rather surprised to find that on my return to prison not one of the prison staff seemed to want to renew the old antagonisms of the past. I was taken in front of many boards, who were sitting to assess me, and my past conduct was nearly always referred to. However this was done in an enquiring manner, typically trying to understand my present attitudes and whether I still had the same hatred for everyone which I had shown in the past. I used to smile and reply that one didn't forget all of the things that I had been through and dismiss them easily. I stated that I just wanted to be left as I was and if I was allowed to get on with my time there would be no problems.

Finally I was called in front of the Governor and told that I was to be sent back to Dartmoor as a Cat. B prisoner. My heart sank upon hearing this news, as I could never imagine being left to forget all that had gone on in that place in the past. However, I just nodded and went back to my cell where I sat and thought long about the life I'd led, of the wasted years and whether Dartmoor would be the same. I wanted to think of the more humorous things that had happened, but there were so very few of them. I did remember the time Jimmy Kensit, the father of Patsy Kensit the film star, was in doing a long sentence. He was known as one of the 'bottle' mob (a top pickpocket). Like most of the bottle mob, Jimmy was chirpy and good humoured. There was a screw who looked like a big yokel but was really a sadistic sod and was always putting someone on report for the most trivial offences. His great day would come every Friday, when he got his wages. In those days they would be paid in pound notes, just a few measly quid. He would take it out of his pocket and hold it up and say, 'That's what I get for locking you lot up.'

We had a word with Jimmy and the following Friday when the screw reached for his money, it wasn't there. He nearly died of shock. Everyone knew and they were nearly all falling about with laughter.

He started to plead, 'Come on, lads, where's my wages? You know I'm not a a bad bloke.'

The PO screamed up at him to get all the prisoners 'banged up' and he shouted back, 'Somebody's pinched my wages, sir.'

The PO couldn't help retorting, 'Yes, I think there might be a thief in this place.'

The big yokel was nearly in tears. He was given his money back but the experience certainly cured him. He never pulled that stunt again.

Would the punishment block be the same? I had visions of that insidious dank cell block and the silence broken only by the clang of keys and the sobbing of guys who had had enough. Would they still be using the cages at the back of the cell block to exercise? Once after I'd been let into the cage for exercise icy sleet started to pelt down. It was all I could do to keep moving and when the screws came to open the cage to let me back into the strongbox, the lock was frozen on the gate. I had to wait shivering until they got a blow lamp to thaw it out.

I was smiling to myself as the memories came flooding back to me. They did everything they could to make things harder but sometimes their best efforts only worked against them.

Every prisoner was allowed a book to read, this being part of the prison rules after the 1940s. If a chaplain, or in some cases a Governor, went into a guy's cell whilst in the punishment block, he would always enquire if the prisoner had something to read. So the screws had a store of books which they considered would be incomprehensible to the average con. They would sling the biggest and thickest books they could find into the cell.

I let them think they were getting one over on me but I read them all, including some pretty heavy material and some very interesting books, like Freud's interpretation of dreams. I had the last laugh when I wrote a petition to the Home Office about my treatment inside the prison. I could hear the Chief Officer saying, 'Somebody must have written that for him. He's used words even the Governor can't understand.' He didn't know that the only book that I'd had in my cell for the past few months was a dictionary. I had a great time with that dictionary. I found a new hobby; taking nursery rhymes, proverbs, etc, and changing the words to mean the same thing. I passed many a boring hour like that.

I wondered if they had done anything about the terrible bathhouse? Its iron baths were stained brown from the peaty water that came directly from the moors, complete with dead insects, pieces of soil and leaves. The walls ran with condensation and pools of dirty water were everywhere. Everyone suffered with athlete's foot as it was so contagious. It was also a meeting place for some pretty sordid and perverted prisoners. The only light relief that would come from that direction was when a particular child molester from Sheffield would come into the bathhouse. All the cons would say, 'Have a look at this beast, this should be a lesson to them all' and someone would pull the towel from around his waist to show where he'd been emasculated by a crowd of women who had caught him with a child in a block of flats.

Things would probably be a lot different now since the Mountbatten Report. There would be more segregation of a lot of prisoners and Rule 43 was the order of the day for all child molesters.

Then I thought of guys like Wanker Green, who was in Dartmoor for many years. I can't remember ever seeing him without at least a black eye. He had apparently molested a gypsy girl and every year there would be a family of gypsies parked near the prison, who would ask the guys on the outside working parties, 'Will you check Wanker Green's cell card and see if his release date is still the same?'

I think they had plans for some kind of reception for him when he was released. I thought I might even hear the result of that on the grapevine when I got back to the 'Moor.

I was back in Dartmoor within a few weeks of seeing the Governor and was immediately met by a few old mates who made me welcome and filled me in with all of the news. I also recognized some of the old screws but from what I could gather, the 'Moor had lost all of its sinister atmosphere. I was interviewed by the Deputy Governor the day after my arrival, and was surprised to find he was one of the Chief Officers from the years gone by.

He said, 'Sit down and let's have a chat.'

No one had ever spoken to me like that before, so I immediately thought that this must be the 'new approach'. But no, he was quite genuine and said to me, 'We try to start off on the right foot here now. Have a look around for a few days to see if there is a job in the prison you fancy doing, then if there is a vacancy, we'll see if we can fix you up.'

I gave this a little thought and I then put my request in for a cleaning job in the education block as I would be mainly on my own and I would have facilities to obtain certain materials for my hobbies and pastimes. So for about a year I went about my life in the 'Moor without any confrontations or incidents. Life in general was more comfortable than in the past: it was warmer following the installation of central heating, there was a new gymnasium, I could watch TV and there were quite a lot of activities going on, which I never dreamed I would see in Dartmoor Prison. I started to use the hobbies room in the education block. As a kid I had always been able to use tools to make things from wood and it wasn't long before I got the hang of it again. With the bit of money I used to earn, I'd buy the raw materials to make a few things to send home to my mother. This worked wonders for the old lady, not only because she liked the things I sent her but also, after all these years, I think a few of her prayers were being answered.

It was at this time that a screw who I knew as 'the Arab'

started coming into the workshop and stopping to have a chat. I was a bit suspicious at first as I had known him for about twenty years and his reputation was not very nice. I stayed very cold towards him when he tried to start a conversation but eventually he put his cards on the table. I couldn't believe my ears when he told me that both he and his wife spent all of their spare time visiting hospitals, raising money for disabled people and kids with various disabilities. He asked me if I would make a few things for a local children's hospital. I agreed and set about the task of making a large dolls' house and garage for the children's ward at Freedom Fields Hospital in Plymouth.

When my models were close to being completed the Governor called me to his office and said that Mr Richards – 'the Arab' – had mentioned to him the things I had been doing in my spare time. He had requested that, when he delivered the models to the hospital, I should accompany him. The Governor then told me that he had been in touch with the Home Office, and they had given the go ahead. It turned out to be a memorable day for me and the event marked a turning point in my life.

There were a few people from the media covering the story of 'The Dartmoor Convict and the Children's Ward'. I met a reporter called Ross Salmon, who I had heard of, and we became quite friendly. He was surprised to learn that prisoners were in a position to carry out hobbies and make toys. We struck up a regular correspondence and with his help we got together an exhibition of prisoners' hobbies, art and crafts. The visitors to the exhibition were amazed at the standard of work that was being shown. Some of the local residents began to take an interest in this work and encouraged the cons to do things for the disabled. A local artist was so impressed by the artistic talent of one of the cons that he requested he should be allowed to visit the prison weekly to work with prisoners with artistic ability. This permission was granted, and it was not long before it seemed that half of the prison population had acquired canvas and easels from some source or other.

It was about this time that Lord Hunt – leader of the 1953 Everest expedition – came to the prison, as Chairman of the Parole Board, to discuss the parole system with certain prisoners. There had been considerable controversy about this system, stemming from the fact that it appeared that only certain cons, mainly white-collar crooks, were benefiting from it. Lord Hunt was very frank and he told us that the Parole Board could not take any chances by releasing bank robbers and serious criminals, as the media would be likely to have a field day if any parolee re-offended. So it was very obvious that I would have to do my time without any hope of parole.

Ross Salmon was still writing to me and he obtained permission to interview me for a radio programme. The broadcast was picked up by another radio show, *Pick of the Week*, and much to my surprise and delight, following the broadcast, I received hundreds of letters from all over the country from all types of people, both encouraging and congratulatory. I answered most of them and also began to correspond more regularly.

Shortly after resigning myself to serving my full stretch, the Governor of Leyhill Prison came to Dartmoor to interview me with the view of getting me transferred to his prison. As I still had three years of my sentence to do, even with remission, I didn't think there was much chance of me moving. At the time, Leyhill was considered to be the most progressive and modern prison in Britain and most of the cons there were white collars, celebrities or bent police. There were also about forty lifers there, who had nearly completed their sentences and were being groomed for release on licence.

To my surprise I was called up about three weeks after the visit by David Atkinson, the Governor of Leyhill, and told I was to be transferred there the following week. In a strange way I was sad to say goodbye to a lot of people in Dartmoor, especially 'the Arab', who had been so helpful to me. Before leaving to go to Leyhill I was allowed to go to his home to meet his wife and to have tea; very different from those bad times years before. I have since been back to Dartmoor and discovered that 'the Arab' had died. His grave looked well cared for and tidy, so his wife is probably still alive. I hope she is well – she was a very nice lady.

When I arrived at Leyhill and completed the reception formalities – clothing, property and personal possessions – the screw in reception said, 'Go up to where the prisoners live, ask about the general routine and come back later, then I'll organize you somewhere to sleep and live.'

I looked at him in astonishment. He left me on the main drive of the prison, looking back to the entrance, and there wasn't even a gate to stop me walking out. I could see cars driving past on the road. I really thought I must be dreaming. But I was soon to learn the value of a system that gives one the responsibility for shaping one's own life and not being told what to do every minute of the day.

However it was not all a bed of roses, there were some strict do's and don'ts. But it was a place where if one wanted to act like a man one would be treated as such.

I soon met a few people who I had known many years before, including Gus Thatcher who was in his twentieth year of a life sentence for the Mitcham Co-op murder. Gus had been sentenced to death and was reprieved just twelve hours before he was due to hang. He had become a playwright and artist but he still seemed a very beaten man when I met him at Leyhill.

One of the first guys I met after arriving was Wally Probyn who I had known for many years. Wally was the guy who had escaped from Durham Prison with John McVicar. Many people had found Wally interesting enough to spend a lot of time writing to him and visiting him, with a view to helping him. But Wally knew that even though the people who wrote to him and visited him were genuine and had a real desire to see him get a break, he had upset so many people in authority over the years that it would not be easy. I think that he eventually made it.

Another fellow prisoner was Barry Brogan, the National Hunt jockey. He was a quiet bloke who seemed pleasant and unassuming and was getting on doing his time. He had apparently been convicted for obtaining money by deception. Although he may have been one of the country's top jockeys he was rather naïve about the way things worked in prison. I remember him being caught with a load of tobacco which he shouldn't have been in possession of and being sent back to a closed prison to complete his sentence.

I also befriended a real adventurer called John Miller. He was tall, good-looking and athletic and had been a Scots

Guardsman. He had also been a mercenary soldier in various parts of the world. I saw a good deal of John when I visited the gym. After a workout we would go for a coffee with a couple of guys who were finishing life sentences. We would spend some time each day socializing and telling stories. I would have thought some of John's tales to be far-fetched if I hadn't seen photographs and letters to prove the veracity of his statements.

John regularly expressed his intention to return to Africa to release the 'dogs of war' from a prison called McKindye. Apparently he knew the guy commanding the rebel forces and he had been assured that any escape would be financed by him. He wanted to meet up with me when we were released in order to put his plan into motion. John thought that with all of the people that I knew, and with his own contacts, the mission would be a doddle. But I kept trying to convince him that I intended going straight and settling down when I was released. That wasn't going to be the last I heard of John.

I soon got settled into the wood-machine shop and met a couple of lifers who were keen to organize a group of guys to join us in making things for children with various degrees of handicap. I gained permission to visit some places that specialized in spina bifida cases and also met a doctor who specialized in them who was very helpful in suggesting things we could make which would be particularly useful to such children.

We became better organized as time went by and with the help of the Governor and staff and with the approval of the Home Office started a Resettlement Group. Eventually we had about forty cons whose sentences ranged from five years to life, going out at weekends as voluntary helpers in various homes, special schools, community centres and private houses, doing a wide variety of jobs. Each of these men went out without supervision, under their own honour, and in the couple of years I was involved, either as Chairman of the Resettlement Group or as a voluntary worker, there was not one complaint or infringement of the rules.

Good times came for the group with the arrival of T. Dan Smith, a politician from Newcastle who, with a chap named Poulson, had been sentenced to six years' imprisonment. I met T. Dan the first day he arrived, an imposing figure, over six feet tall. We were playing Scrabble in the billet and he joined in. We got chatting and within a few days I began to recognize in Dan a very strong character.

We would sit together talking of our past lives and Dan would tell me of his early years when he would take part in the forerunners to the early union meetings and the police would come to break them up. As the police horses would crash into the meetings Dan would always be singled out as the tallest man there. Years later, when he attained his office in local government, he interviewed a senior police officer in Newcastle. He recognized the officer as being the one who was always the first in with the batons and took some pleasure in reminding him of those days. He was happy to see that the police officer blushed.

Dan's case was one of the big trials in the early seventies – a case of corruption in the awarding of contracts to rebuild Newcastle. A lot of politicians were quaking when the case unfolded but most of the big names involved escaped prosecution and Dan and the architect Poulson took the flak and the punishment.

After hearing what we were doing in the Resettlement Group he expressed a desire to help. It was the best thing that happened to the group, for Dan had not only considerable artistic talent, but also many friends outside. I wrote to many of these people, with his encouragement, and they helped us by providing the raw materials we needed for our projects.

Dan was tireless and kept everyone on their toes. He was a leading light in all of the activities with the prison, including the drama group, where one of his leading men was Leslie Grantham, later to become famous as Dirty Den in *EastEnders*, who was then finishing a life sentence. Dan was involved with the debating society, where we used to debate with teams from Bristol and Cardiff universities, as well as the Round Table. I spent an enjoyable, enriching and memorable time with him.

One day, entirely out of the blue, I received a pleasant surprise: I was told that I had been granted parole. I still had a few weeks to go, after this news, and Dan spent much of this time contacting many of his outside friends to see what help they could give to me after my release. From these introductions I met Harold Evans, who was then editor of the *Sunday Times*, and also Sir Monty Finniston, then the boss at British Steel. Through him, and other friends of T. Dan, I obtained a very good job.

CHAPTER TWENTY

Going Straight

Going to see Sir Monty Finniston at the British Steel headquarters in Victoria Street at the behest of T. Dan Smith was an important moment in my life. First I was made very welcome and, as with Harold Evans, I found people didn't want to dismiss me because of my appalling past. They seemed to take notice of what Dan had to say and were full of constructive ideas as to how the continuation of my apparent resettlement was going to progress. The first thing Sir Monty did was to ring some friends from Political and Economic Planning to see if there was anyone interested in meeting me with a view to providing employment.

Within a few days I had a letter from PEP asking me to go to a meeting with one of the country's leading food manufacturing groups, where I was to have a very good interview with the managing director. I was asked how I would go about tackling problems of social differences in industry. I put forward a view of the way we tackled similar differences in the class system which existed in the penal system at the time. I argued that if you wanted something to work for the good of everyone, using the example that I was familiar with, namely the Resettlement Group, where there were bank robbers, gangsters, murderers, fraudsters, petty criminals, bent policemen and ex-lawyers all pulling together with one common aim, then it was essential to establish the correct attitudes and focus upon the tasks required, without even thinking of what background your fellow prisoners came from. I seemed to have impressed the boss because I was offered a job immediately. It was a very good job with a salary to match.

I went to my mother's house (my father had died many years earlier) and said, 'I'm in my forties now and I've just started my first proper job.' There were tears in the old girl's eyes and I knew she was very happy for me. Well, I set about my job, which I enjoyed, although there was a fair bit of obstruction from some of the middle management. I think that part of the problem was that I couldn't talk about my past and they sensed that I had something to hide. Perhaps if I could have been more open with them they would have accepted me better. I've learned not to be ashamed of my past and, although I don't volunteer anything, if I'm asked I tell the truth. I've found that most people are OK about it and some are intrigued and want to know more.

I managed to get the social club operational with the help of one of the Asian managers and an Irish worker. We had some marvellous social evenings, and established a football team which had regular fixtures with other factories in the north of England. The friendly banter of the supporters from the various teams wasn't about the players' origins but was centred on the north v. south cultural divide. I stayed at that job until I felt I was ready to start my own business. I had a meeting with the managing director and was given a generous handshake.

I was now rather at a loss as to what to do with myself.

I didn't really want to stay in London, as I felt I had done very well and seemed to be putting my past life completely behind me, but there was always the chance if I stayed in the City that I would start to bump into old associates and gradually be drawn back into the false glamour of the underworld. I decided to go back to Bristol where I had made a lot of friends whilst engaged in my work with resettlement from Leyhill Prison.

At first it was lovely to meet some of the people that I had befriended and had inspired me into taking a different direction in my life, but I had to get settled into a home, employment and generally do all the things that a person does when he decides to keep on the 'straight and narrow'. But although I had some pretty good references from my employers in London, I didn't find it easy to get started. I then remembered a name from the old days, Terry O'Brien. I had heard that he had left London years ago and started an entirely new life in Bristol, and that he had become very successful in business. I thought I would try to find him and see what would come of it.

It was simple, I just looked in the phone book and within a matter of hours I was meeting T.O.B. for the first time in nearly twenty years. Not only that, I was meeting his family, Miriam and son Michael, all of whom I was very grateful to as they were to become my closest friends over the next year or so and made it a lot easier to get started in a new environment.

I worked for Terry and Michael in their business as a kind of 'Jack of all trades'. I even did the signwriting over one of their premises, which I was very proud of as it stood out for anyone who came into the Bristol area via Temple

Meads Station to see. I not only worked for them but socialized with them and became one of the family. It was inevitable, however, that I would start to bump into people from my past life. Strangely enough I never once met anyone that didn't appear to be happy to see that life was going well for me.

Michael liked to go to the casino at the weekend for a meal and a little flutter, and he always invited me. I got to know the boss of the casino, Joe Firetto, who was a gentleman. He knew of my past life but never mentioned it. I often think of all of the characters that I met whilst I was in Bristol. You'd have to go a long way before you could find a nicer lot of people. They were all so obliging and friendly that I miss them and often have a hankering to go and visit them all again.

I had a very pleasant and unexpected surprise one evening when I went out for dinner with a few friends. I was in a very popular restaurant when a guy sitting at the next table with his back to me turned around when he heard me speaking and said, 'Eric, what brings you to this part of the world?'

It was Johnny Quirk. The last time I had seen John was in Dartmoor Prison at the time I had been transferred to Leyhill. I had got to know him very well in Dartmoor through my old friend Dudley, who John used to work for. John had been sentenced to five years for an affray in a club in Bristol and when he was allocated to Dartmoor Dudley got in touch with me and asked me to watch out for him when he arrived and see that he was looked after. I would keep an eye on the list of people who had been allocated to Dartmoor each month and one day John's name was on it. I found an empty cell near mine and arranged for him to be located there when he arrived. John was very quiet when he first came in. I introduced myself and could see straight away that he had a problem. I was soon to find out that John was seriously into drugs, heroin and such, and was having quite a problem fighting the addiction. It was a credit to him the way he finally did beat it. He was to become one of the most respected people in the prison, very intelligent and with a great sense of humour. It was a pleasant surprise when I met him in the restaurant and we started to fill each other in with all of the news over the past years.

Sadly I began to realize that John was back into drugs and I hated to see what it was doing to him. I would bump into him now and again over the next couple of years and would see he was deteriorating in health. He would tell me of friends of his that had died as a result of the habit. I felt that there would only be one end for John, but I'm happy to write that after many years of not seeing him, I went to a reunion party in London a year or so ago and he was there, looking great. He had eventually beaten the thing and was now lecturing young people on the pitfalls of the drug scene. He was even going back, voluntarily, to prisons to talk to young offenders. I could see John was a very happy man again.

I got a bit of a surprise when I arrived back in Bristol after a weekend away. Michael O'Brien had left a message for me to go to a certain pub in Clifton to meet a guy who had come from London to see me urgently. When I arrived there was my old friend from Leyhill, John Miller. He looked very well, tanned and smartly dressed. I was pleased to see him as I had enjoyed his company when we had been in prison together. But I couldn't believe it when he took some papers and photographs from his pocket. The papers were contracts with a film company (belonging to his partner) which he used to impress the company that hired him the light aircraft and other equipment he needed to implement the elaborate plan to kidnap Biggs. It was when John showed me some photographs, recently taken of himself, Biggsy and a couple of other people, that I realized that John really meant business. That attempt failed at the last minute but John was not one to give up easily. I had almost forgotten the whole thing when I saw a news flash on TV that Ronnie Biggs had been kidnapped from Brazil. I eagerly followed the story over the next few days and sure enough there were the pictures of my old pal John with Biggsy being flashed all over the world. John got him as far as Barbados but the Brazilian government insisted on Ronnie's return and back he went.

But it was time to look at a more mundane future for myself. With the help of a bank loan I was able to start my own club. Because of my background I could not hold a club licence so I had to take a partner. I teamed up with a very nice guy who was a hotelier, and went into business.

We had a very successful start and I was quite happy for my partner to hold the lease on the premises. He was younger than me, only in his thirties, and for a year or so we had a very good business relationship. We paid back the bank loan before the first year was up and had each just taken delivery of a new car.

But my partner had matrimonial problems. He'd split with his wife and although he had a new girlfriend living at the hotel with him, he couldn't get his wife out of his mind. She was also restricting his association with his young son and he began to get very morose and cynical. Then one day I got a great shock. My partner had phoned me at the club about midday and he seemed in a pretty good mood, but about an hour later his girlfriend rang to say he'd gone to his car, with the Hoover and a blanket, and gassed himself.

His family inherited the business, leaving me with nothing and I was financially worse off than when I first started. I began to drink and sit around in bars going over things, when I decided to look up an old friend of mine whilst visiting Manchester for a football match. This friend mentioned Derek who used to play with the old Dreamers band in the sixties. I'd had some nice times with Derek, who was now a publican in Manchester, and I thought I'd pop in to see him and his wife. He was surprised to see me after all those years and we went to a club the next evening for some dinner. There we met another old friend, who was originally from London, but was now also a publican in Manchester. I decided to spend a couple of weeks there to sort myself out and, in no time at all, I was booked into Jimmy Donnelly's hotel where I ended up staying for a year.

Manchester and the Quality Street Gang

I met Jimmy Donnelly (also known as Jimmy the Weed) soon after arriving in Manchester. People always ask me, 'Why do they call him Jimmy the Weed? Is it true that if you do business with him he always has a weed at the wages at the end of the deal?' Now I've always had good deals with Jimmy so I'll have to go along with his explanation. He once showed me a photograph of himself and a few of the chaps when he was young and he looked pretty weedy then.

But alhough he is small in stature he has the heart of a lion. One evening, recently, Jimmy and I, along with our wives and friends, were invited to a big dinner/cabaret-cum-charity show at the Piccadilly Hotel. The actor Mark McManus, who plays Taggart, and his wife Marion were two of our guests and we were all having a great time.

Anyone who needed to go to the gents or ladies' room had to leave the main hall, where the show was going on, and pass a lounge outside one of the two bars. Apparently everyone who had to pass this spot came back complaining of two guys who were sitting there hurling insults and making lewd gestures at passers-by. I thought that if any of our company made a move to go out I would accompany

250

them but Jimmy had already pre-empted me. He casually strolled outside to where the two pests were sitting. One of them shouted 'Hey waiter!' to Jimmy, who had just spent about £1,000 on a new dinner jacket and all the trimmings. Jimmy said, 'So I look like a waiter, do I? Then I'd better give you some service.' With that he knocked the pair of them out, came strolling back to the table with a grin and asked the waiter to have them removed from the hotel.

Jimmy was a member of the Quality Street Gang, a group of men accused by the press of being behind most of Manchester's major crime. The press are very careful not to mention them by name as they are largely businessmen – men of some substance. They are also very tough boys but I never saw any of them take a liberty.

The name 'the Quality Street Gang' made the news during the John Stalker–Kevin Taylor affair. Jack Tricket, a prominent Manchester boxing promoter, speaking on *World in Action*, used it to describe Kevin Taylor's friends. The name was used very much tongue-in-cheek by people who were jealous of the success of the QSG members but it stuck and made the association of these men seem more sinister than it actually was.

The beginnings of the QSG go back to the 1960s, when Jimmy the Weed and his friends were dabbling in the scrap metal business. They progressed into construction and were soon making plenty of money and socializing in all of the well-known nightclubs. The doormen of these clubs were often friends of the QSG and worked with them in their day jobs. As a result, when local drunks or would-be tough guys tried to flex their muscles, any QSG members around would weigh in to give the doormen a hand in sorting out any trouble. It became fashionable for club owners to mention that the QSG were regulars at their club, thus ensuring themselves trouble-free evenings. After an incident at the Wilton club in 1962, when a noted underworld figure of the day was put in hospital, the QSG were seen as pretty fearless fighting men.

Before the formation of the QSG there were many respected individuals that the criminal fraternity would look up to, or borrow money from to set up some illegal scam or robbery. I met most of these people over the years as there was a good rapport between the London and Manchester underworld figures. One of the most outstanding was Bob McDermott, who was as well known in the capital as he was in Manchester and would always be seen at the ringside with his entourage at the big sporting events. Bob made a very good living from the barrows. Most guys in the fruit and veg game worked for Bob, or at least borrowed money for stock from him, with a small interest attached.

Bob was the proprietor of the Cellar, a club situated in the centre of Manchester and famous with gamblers nationwide. It was frequented by everyone that gambled or had reason to seek help from the many underworld figures that always seemed to be in attendance. It was here that I first started to hear of the QSG and the impression given was far from sinister – they were spoken of as tough, fun-loving guys who all seemed to be quite wealthy. One got the feeling that they were respected because although they were tough they never threw their weight about.

Deno's in the centre of Manchester was one of the most popular clubs in Britain and most cabaret artists have worked there at some time. There were many fortunes won and lost at Deno's gaming tables, and many thousands of bottles of champagne consumed during its heyday. A lot of its glamour came from the fact that the QSG made it their headquarters for a long time.

They also frequented the Cabaret club in Oxford Road. This was owned by Bill Benny, an ex-wrestler who died whilst making love to one of the many beautiful women who used the club. This particular *femme fatale* became well known in Manchester for accomplishing a deed many had attempted unsuccessfully, and without using anything except her technique.

The head doorman at the Cabaret was Billy Ingham, an ex-boxer who was to become a very good friend of mine (he died recently). Billy told me that he always looked forward to the QSG coming to the club as he could relax while they were there.

Another great Manchester character was Bobby Crichley who made his money in the used car trade. At one time there was a spate of forged car insurance certificates going around and the local police inspector detailed two young coppers to go to Bobby's site and turn him over for the bent certificates. As the two young coppers pulled into the site Bobby strolled out of his office to greet them. He was a shrewd guy, as well as being a great joker, and knew exactly what he could get away with.

'What can I do for you two gentlemen?' he asked.

'We've come about the bent certificates,' one of the coppers said.

Bobby immediately responded, 'I'm sorry, chaps, but they've been so popular I've sold them all. But if you leave me your names and addresses I'll see you both get one from the next batch.'

From construction Jimmy moved on to become a publican, hotelier and nightclub owner. He helped a few people on their way and as a consequence the police kept a very watchful eye on him. But though he was arrested on numerous occasions they could never make their charges stick.

The funniest week I had with Jimmy arose out of a tragic situation which forced him to leave the country very quickly. He was wanted for questioning about the shooting of a man called John Stones in a Manchester pub and Jimmy decided to leave the country for his own good. I received a call from his brother one evening asking me to meet Jimmy. He was arranging a passport and other documents in order to slip out of the country. At the moment, his brother said, Jimmy was with a make-up artist from a TV company, inventing a disguise. But would I meet him in a pub in Stockport later, as there were a few things he wanted me to arrange for him before he left the country?

When I arrived at the pub Jimmy was standing with his brother at the bar. He faced me and asked, 'What's the disguise like?'

'Well,' I said tactfully, 'I knew it was you because you were standing with your brother and I expected to see you anyway. But otherwise I don't think I would have recognized you.'

This seemed to reassure him and we had a couple of drinks while we plotted Jimmy's disappearance. As we walked out to the car park an old pal of ours was just arriving with his wife. He immediately greeted us all by our names, then said to Jimmy, 'What have you got that funny hat on for, Jim?'

I burst out laughing, while Jimmy muttered, 'I've just bunged a guy £200 for this disguise and everyone knows me.' But everything was all right in the end and I think Jimmy could still hear me laughing as he went through passport control a few days later.

I'd also met a woman in Manchester who was spending all her time with a Lancashire group who did voluntary work with the disabled. I popped in to see her now and again and would help with little things but I soon realized that what I'd done in prison was easy in comparison to the dedication given by people who help voluntarily every day of their lives. They are really special and I found I was seeing less and less of them as time went by. I did go back to Leyhill to visit a friend and found that T. Dan Smith was still making the odd trip back to encourage the men we left behind. It was then that I realized why he had stood out as being one of the more special people in my life.

By this time I had become involved in the wholesale business with a few friends. I had a flat in Prestwick and was living with a girl who was the manageress of the Queens club. Life had taken on a new meaning for me and I had stopped looking back at what might have been and had decided to enjoy myself and make new friends. When my girlfriend told me she was pregnant I was overjoyed. We moved into a house with her two sons aged nine and seven.

I was frequenting the Queens club a lot of the time, where I bumped into old friends from my gambling days as well as the odd policeman. In fact, it was in the Queens club that a senior police officer approached me about Jimmy. His alleged victim, Stones, had refused to make a statement about his shooting and the police had decided to drop the matter. 'Tell Jimmy he can come home,' the officer said. I did, although Jimmy took some persuading that it really was safe.

Kevin Taylor was one of the faces I knew quite well from the sixties and he seemed to be doing well in business. He was dabbling in local politics and always had a friendly word when we came across each other. He was to be caught up in the Stalker affair, when the Assistant Chief Constable was accused of socializing with Kevin who in turn was accused both of fraud and of being friends of the QSG. The case collapsed in court but in the mean time Taylor and Stalker had both suffered.

I met John Stalker in the directors' box at Maine Road, Manchester City's ground. I was introduced by Doug Welsby, who had known Stalker since his early days on the beat. Doug, who was a licensee for over thirty years, said Stalker was the straightest copper he'd ever known. When the storm broke and Stalker resigned, it reminded me of one particular occasion in Blackpool in the sixties. The police were taking considerable notice of everything I was doing, although I was only socializing with some friends. Nevertheless, word had got out that we were into rackets of some description. The headlines in the papers were 'High-powered Gangster Using Motorways to Commute'. As a consequence, every time we went out we were escorted. The police were making it very difficult for us to go anywhere, as well as making things difficult for any licensee who served us. At that time I was living with a girl who was in showbiz and the police even went backstage to tell her that I was an ex-convict. So I devised a plan.

I had noticed that some senior police officers would be present at the top social functions, such as charity shows. Two of my friends, Steve and Jimmy Clark, the American dancers and entertainers, were giving an end of season party for all their friends in showbiz at the Win Moreth club in Blackpool. Everyone was going to be there so I asked them to invite some senior police officers and their wives. I then arranged to have my own photographer at the party in addition to the official one.

Steve had seated the police at my table, which made for a nice cosy picture. Naturally during the course of the evening I also asked a few of the wives to dance. I ended up with some very friendly photographs. From then on I was allowed to socialize without any interruption.

The Stalker affair meant that the police were taking an extra interest in the QSG at that time. Jimmy was harassed so much that he decided to leave Manchester. He now lives happily on the coast overlooking the sea in quiet retirement. I asked him if he would go back to live in Manchester and in reply he picked up a Manchester newspaper and pointed to the headline 'Three Men Gunned Down in City Gang War'.

'That sort of thing happens every week now,' he said. 'I think I'll just grow old gracefully.'

Although a lot of the Manchester underworld figures that I know do show respect, I find from talking to them that they feel crime in their city is taking the same route as in London. There is a consensus of opinion that the drug scene is responsible for crime sinking to new depths – so much so that the ordinary citizen can see the average robber as being fairly respectable in comparison. There have always been the footpads and the highwaymen but the horrific attacks on the old, the rapes and apparently motiveless stabbings are something new. When Jimmy the Weed tells me about the early days of the QSG it seems almost harmless in comparison.

Quite soon after meeting Jimmy the Weed I realized that he had friends in most of the major cities throughout Great Britain. I often travelled with Jimmy to various functions – maybe a boxing event, or a charity cabaret or just a business trip. We spent quite a lot of time in Glasgow, where I met a few old friends as well as making new ones.

The Glasgow I knew in the fifties is a far cry from the place it is now. The days of the Gorbals when all the differences between gangs or individuals were settled with a razor-slashing are long gone. One still does hear of local tough guys cutting each other but in the main the major fall outs are now over money or area supremacy and are dealt with more ruthlessly. The weapons used today are guns.

There has been a big power struggle going on in the Glasgow underworld which has become more intense since the death of Arthur Thompson, the acknowledged leader for a quarter of a century. One very tough young guy has recently been acquitted of the murder of Arthur Thompson Jnr. but the sons of other well-known ex-villains have ambitions to take over the lucrative position of Scotland's crime boss.

I had rather an odd experience whilst visiting Glasgow

one evening. My wife and I had been invited out to dinner and we were taken first to a very nice cocktail bar to meet some friends who were to join us for the meal. We were all sitting quietly enjoying a drink just waiting for the last two of our company to arrive, when there was a terrifying noise of skidding and crashing and the whole front of the bar came falling in. A lorry was half in and half out of the bar about eight feet from where we were sitting. On the back of the wagon was a guy with a machine-gun. It looked like something out of an old gangster movie. Then one of our company jumped up and started to remonstrate with the driver and the guy with the gun. The two guys were soon apologizing and saying to our friend that they didn't know he used that particular bar. They obviously had some grudge with the owners but they just backed the lorry out and drove off. We finished our drinks and were trying to make light of things to calm down our wives who were a little unnerved by the incident. Our other two friends arrived and were surprised to see us walking out past a car that had been rammed up against a wall next to the shattered bar front. The only thing we ever heard of that incident again was when someone phoned our friends' house to say that they were sorry for upsetting the evening out.

Over the years I've met quite a few people from Scotland, mainly from either Glasgow or Edinburgh. The majority of them have been either sportsmen or underworld figures but there has been the odd ordinary businessman. Whatever their particular profession I've found them to be reliable, honest with each other, and very hospitable. There is always the exception to the rule, but in general I've had some great moments in Scotland and also some quite humorous times. I remember the night I was invited to a boxing dinner at the Barrowlands in Glasgow. Every dignitary in the city was there along with just about anyone that had a reputation. Now it was quite well known that the Barrowlands had been the place where many of the top villains had earned their reputations as young men at the Saturday night dances. It had become quite notorious through the many books and articles that had been written about it. I was sitting at one of the long tables with a lot of smart-looking guys all dressed in dinner jackets. There were champagne corks popping and everything looked like a gentleman's night out until the MC started to deliver his welcoming words. He first greeted all of the dignitaries and personalities, some by their titles or in the case of the police by their rank.

He then said, 'As you all know, this is the very first official boxing event ever to be held at the Barrowlands.' Then he glanced towards the table I had been invited to join and added, 'But I make a special welcome to some of my friends who have been the unofficial champions of the "Barras".' This broke the ice and everyone then nodded at each other with a grin. It turned out to be another great night in Glasgow.

Jimmy still meets up with some of his old friends from Glasgow when they come down to Blackpool for the 'Scots fortnight'. Jim is able to report on how old mutual friends are doing, now resident on the Costa del Sol – or the Costa del Crime as it is known. That particular part of Spain between Fuengirola and Marbella seems to attract most of the people wanted for various crimes in Britain. Once out there a lot of the old antagonisms are forgotten out of respect for each others' predicament.

Jimmy is frequently asked to deliver a message to certain of his friends in Spain, to tell them that it is OK to come home as the 'straighteners' have been put in and they are no longer wanted.

I've often sat outside a bar in Los Boliches from about 9 p.m. to 6 a.m. with a dozen men and their wives or girlfriends, most of whom are wanted for a variety of crimes in London, Manchester or Glasgow. Anyone passing would think we were a group of businessmen on a break away from the office. No one discusses their crimes. They are common knowledge within the fraternity but the subject is taboo.

There are also one or two phoneys who have managed to ingratiate themselves into the company. These are the kind of people who are always on the fringes, who have gleaned a lot of information about the various underworld figures and can talk about them with apparent inside information. They are one of the reasons I have never wanted to spend much time there. In fact, I have noticed that the men wanted for major crimes keep themselves mainly out of the limelight and socialize at private dinner parties and such where the conversation is more constructive.

I think that the advent of the Spanish sanctuary for the British criminal has helped forge the links between the underworlds of the major British cities. Crime has become a very big industry and is now a lot more sophisticated. A guy from Glasgow can slip on to the shuttle in the morning, fly to London and plot with his Cockney counterpart, have some lunch and be back home in time for tea.

The difference between London and the other major cities lies in the vast size of the capital which means that there is room for a number of accepted 'governors'. Most of them seem to live without clashing. I think the general public in the more deprived areas of London take a certain pride in their local villains, especially if they are described in the press as 'London crime bosses'. It becomes a talking point. And most people realize that when you have some pretty heavy people about it cuts down on the sort of crime that affects the ordinary hard-working folk. The kind of characters who break in to working-class homes realize they may be breaking in to the house of the mother or relative of the biggest villain on the manor, so in a way their existence has its own policing effect.

CHAPTER TWENTY-TWO

Back to Crime
and Strangeways

I had now settled down happily with my girlfriend and was getting on with my business. I had moved my premises to the outskirts of Blackpool and for a while things seemed to be going quite well. Then a few people started to get behind with payments for the goods they had bought on credit. I was forced to extend my credit facilities with the bank. I struggled on, hoping things would get better but all the while the bills were mounting. I started to feel that I was a failure – that no matter what I did, nothing would go right for me. To add to my worries, I had just become the father of a son and I felt that I would rather go to prison for a short while than condemn my family to a life of drudgery and debt.

I took the easy way out and decided to get a few quid together and shut up shop. I sold up all my stock and ordered more and then just waited for the inevitable. The police finally came and told me that it was illegal to sell stock for less than it was worth and then not pay the suppliers. I replied that I knew this but customers hadn't paid me what they owed and so I didn't have the money. They started to explain about calling in the receiver when

I interrupted. 'I know all about that, but I decided to take the easy way out.'

'You call this the easy way?' They couldn't believe what they were hearing. But I felt a kind of calmness, as if everything would be OK. I ended up back in court, charged with fraud amounting to £300,000.

Although I didn't have very much, I had a bit put by and as I thought I would probably be going back to prison, I decided to take my girl and little son on a holiday before having to face the music. We went off for a couple of weeks to Malaga on the Costa del Sol, and it wasn't long before I was bumping into a lot of old friends.

I met Bob and his wife who were running a nice club in Benelmadna. Then Maurice, who had a nice little bar that was a meeting place for all the chaps. My old mate Curly King turned up there one night looking twenty years younger than he was. Then a pal of mine for many years heard that I was in Los Boliches and came looking for me, with his new wife. This was Ronnie Knight who was wanted in Britain in connection with the £6 million Security Express robbery. At the time, I was quite pleased to see him and we had a couple of days together. We went to his villa for dinner and on another evening went out there for a barbecue. I was sorry to have to leave, knowing I was probably facing a bit more time in the nick, but I wouldn't have changed places with any one of the boys who had to live there; they were chancing many years in jail when they got back to this country.

So I came back to face the music and found I still had a few weeks to go before my case came up. I went to London to watch the Bruno v. Bugner fight at White Hart Lane and joined some friends afterwards at the Blondes club, run by George Best. There was the good old smiling face of Curly King again. We decided to go to Langhams restaurant for a meal. I said to Curly, 'When I saw you in Spain I thought you were on the run.'

'No,' he said, 'I haven't been in trouble for years and I'm glad to see you've been out of it yourself.'

I didn't have the heart to tell him I was on bail waiting to go up on a fraud charge.

Finally the case started. There was no point in messing around, I was done 'bang to rights', so I pleaded guilty and was sentenced to two and a half years. In the old days that would have meant doing a certain twenty months, with good behaviour. But in the present day there was a good chance of being out in ten months with parole. So I thought, I've been lucky and it's up to me to get on with it, keep my mouth shut and get home as quickly as I can.

But that was easier said than done. I was sent to Strangeways and the minute I got in there and smelt the prison smell I thought, What have you done? I knew that my wife Carole had never experienced the stigma of having a relation in prison – and I knew that she would not get used to it very easily. I was not too happy on my own behalf either, particularly after trying so hard to go straight.

I was in a prison that had had for years the worst reputation among prisoners. Everyone hated the thought of being sent there and it was common knowledge that if it ever ignited into a riot, it would be one of the worst in the history of prison riots in this country. I remember the stories of the Hull rioters being brought to Strangeways to get the 'treatment'. From the moment they arrived they ran thé gauntlet of brutality. People often ask me what causes men to riot and go on a rampage of the kind that happened in Manchester's Strangeways Prison in 1990. There is no easy answer to that question but I do have a view based upon my own experiences.

The first thing one must remember is that any man who decides to riot knows beforehand that he is going to have to take some lengthy punishment when it is all over. So before he takes up the cudgels he has to have been brought to a point where he is past caring what the consequences are likely to be.

Therefore in searching for the causes one needs to look deep into the whole system. Some of the complaints may appear to be trivial to those who have not had their freedom taken away. But when you add them all together you will find what it is that ultimately causes a person to snap.

The things that matter most to prisoners are usually food, visits and the ease with which they are able to change cells. One of the greatest causes of personal misery for most prisoners is the guys they are forced to do their time with. There is a considerable amount of bullying as well as the usual tensions you would expect when you have possibly three blokes with very different personalities locked up together in a space ten feet by eight feet for up to twenty-three hours every day.

You try to regulate your bodily functions so as to use the toilet when you are unlocked for exercise or slopping out. However, this becomes nearly impossible, especially in the evening when you are locked up at 7 p.m., following slopping out, and then face the prospect of twelve hours before the cell door is opened again. Everyone knows what is going to happen if you ring your bell after you have been locked up for the evening. The first time you ring your bell you will hear the night duty screw shout, 'Use your pot.' The pot is a plastic bucket (in the old days it was a chamber pot). If a new prisoner goes into a cell where the bucket has been used by the previous con for any length of time the stench which hits him upon lifting the lid immediately starts him wondering what kind of experience he is going to have to get through.

As well as the bucket, you become aware of the smell of body odour the first minute you walk into the cell. There are no such things as hygiene and cleanliness inspectors within the prison. It makes me smile when I hear of restaurant owners being fined heavily by the courts for lack of hygiene. Ask any ex-con about the stench of slopping out, the cockroaches and the parcels of shit that are thrown out of the cell windows, to name just a few of the health hazards that exist in any prison.

Then there are the prison officers. There are some reasonably decent blokes among them, but most have their hands tied by the rules and regulations. Prison officers are taught not to trust any prisoner, so suspicion always plays a part in the relationships between officer and con.

Prison officers that are new to the job are given conducted tours round various prisons wearing their civilian clothes. They look just like anyone's next-door neighbour, and I know from many of the conversations I have had with these newcomers that they either come into the prison service for a secure job with a house provided or they think they have something to offer to the penal system. I really don't think that there are many who arrive with any sadistic thoughts or ideas about running the lives of the people beneath them. But you can tell the type of screw he's going to be by the nature of the screw who shows him the ropes when he first comes into the job. He might well come from his training establishment with all the good will in the world, but that can all too easily be forgotten when he starts the job. True, the influences could work the other way, but it only needs one or two bad staff to upset the whole of a prison. This is particularly so if they are senior or principal officers who would normally be expected to stop other screws taking advantage of their position to make things difficult for certain cons. It is easy to see the signs of abuse by the number of complaints, cases such as a bloke smashing up his cell furniture or, in extreme circumstances, the suicide of a prisoner.

Another major problem is boredom, with very little work being done in the prisons. Some cons can get a job where they are paid enough to enable them to buy tobacco to last for a week, whilst the rest are given an allowance to last just a day or so. This creates great resentment and encourages borrowing which results in guys fighting, or worse, to the extent that prisoners ask to go on Rule 43 – complete segregation.

Since most of the mental hospitals have been closed there are thousands of people who have known no other life except for an institution, being put out into society to fend for themselves. Tragically many of these people have ended up in prison and have been used by some officers to get their own back on certain cons who they do not see eye to eye with. Moving the poor chap, who may not be able to control his body functions or may have some other unsociable habits, into the cell of a con the screw doesn't like can have distressing results.

There are also many cases of screws using their pet hardmen to chastise the guys who know their rights and try to exercise them. They, the landing officers, seem to get what is commonly known in prison speak as 'My No 1' – generally a recidivist, who takes a pleasure in being the butt of the officers' insults. He's the type who always manages to be in possession of a number of porn magazines so his landing officer therefore always has something to read when he has no other work to do. He is always ready to pick a fight with somebody that doesn't see eye to eye with the landing officer. He always ensures that the landing officer has got a cup of tea and is made aware of everything that is going on inside the prison.

Up until the industrial troubles, when the Prison Officers' Association (POA) came through their fight with management and succeeded in becoming more powerful, a prisoner could always make an application to see the Governor. He didn't have to explain the nature of his application and was immediately in the Governor's office after adjudication and was able to make his request or complaint. If it was a normal request that fell within the rules of the prison it was usually granted. If, however, it was a complaint against a prison officer or dissatisfaction with the food or something outside the rules, he would be warned immediately of the consequences of not proving his complaint. It was up to him to either pursue his complaint or let the governor deal with it.

But now you make your application and are then brought in front of the senior officer to state your complaint.

He then decides whether it warrants going in front of the Chief Officer or Assistant Governor. You very rarely get to see the governor himself, and in the mean time the word has gone around that you are a trouble maker and then your problems really start. In the case of a guy who is not able to take the pressure, he is likely to do something silly like smashing up his cell furniture. He will then at least see the Governor at adjudication, but the chances are that he will be manhandled on the way to the punishment block. The sounds of cell furniture being smashed and the subsequent beating create a very strained atmosphere throughout the prison. It then only takes the smallest spark to ignite a very serious situation.

It is quite obvious to me that the prison authorities felt that they dealt wrongly with the Strangeways mutiny and that they should have been allowed to storm the place the day after it started. I think that would have resulted in a larger loss of life. I know that people will say that there were some very serious injuries inflicted in the Strangeways riot but there were many injuries in that place, and in other prisons, long before April 1990 and I believe that there will be many more injuries to sustain on both sides unless the whole penal system is looked at critically.

After the Strangeways affair there were several flashpoints in various prisons around the country and it became the policy for these small uprisings or defiant rebellions to be brought under control swiftly, regardless of what force was used. This has given the POA the idea that it can carry on as usual. Well, I can assure them that if they don't use the strength of their union to ensure that there is a complete overhaul of the whole penal system, there will be an uprising which will make the Strangeways affair look like a playground fight.

There is a vital need to try to reduce the prison population and then to start resettlement courses as well as doing something about the hygiene and getting prisoners out of their cells into some kind of work where they are able to earn enough money to pay for some of the small luxuries of life. I am aware that there is a certain element of prisoners who must be kept in secure prisons and there are also a considerable number who must be shown that other law-abiding people have to be protected. There is, however, one very obvious way to begin to reduce the prison population, by stopping the practice of sending people with mental illnesses to jail. Treat them for what they are, sick people who have no place in prison. I am sure that it would be much cheaper to look for further reforms than it would be to spend the millions it is costing to repair the damage to Strangeways and the other places that have been partly destroyed.

I knew exactly what to do the minute I got in to Strangeways. I was put into D Wing and, as soon as I got to the cell, I saw it was fitted out for three prisoners. I had never had to experience this overcrowding before and I didn't know how I was going to react to it. But the gods were on my side. There was just one guy in the cell when I got there and he'd only arrived the day before me. He'd never been inside before and was pretty scared about what was going on. So he was pleased to meet someone who knew the ropes. The very next day we received another cell mate, a boxer, who had got himself into a fight outside the ring and had been sentenced to two months. They were both clean, and we made the place as habitable as possible.

After a couple of days the PO called me to his office and said, 'I've been looking at your record and I don't see the point of keeping you here. Would you like to go to Kirkham Open Prison?' He got an immediate affirmative from me and I settled down to wait the couple of weeks before going to the open nick. A few days later, I was walking in the exercise yard when a guy came over and said, 'Are you Eric Mason?'

'Yes,' I replied.

'You may remember me, I'm Billy Cox,' he said.

I remembered Billy as a kid; he was an adopted son of Connie Whitehead.

'What are you doing up here?' I asked.

Then he told me all about a scam he'd been involved in.

'Seeing as you've only got twelve months, put down for Kirkham. You'll be better off,' I suggested.

He did this immediately and a couple of days later the PO called me up again and said, 'We've got to put you back a bit for Kirkham as there's a new bloke who's just applied for the open nick. As he's a first offender, he's going in your place, but you're top of the list for next month.'

I don't have to tell you who it was who went in my place! But I knew that I had more chance than Billy of getting through that extra month as he was nearly cracking up with all the things that were happening to him. He was dying to knock the No.1 out, and as I knew Billy was a good boxer, he would have done the business on the guy and got himself a lot of grief. Also all the screams and shouts that were coming from the punishment block below our cells were a bit unsettling, particularly for newcomers. It was a relief to be going to Kirkham the following month.

As soon as I arrived at Kirkham Prison, I met Billy Cox, who had settled in and made a few mates. Although Kirkham was a pretty easy place as prisons go, it had many petty little rules that were more irritating than intimidating. Most of the staff who I came into contact with were pretty decent people, but there was still the odd one or two who would take advantage of the little bit of authority that they had. Overall, however, it was the type of con who was in there that made life in Kirkham difficult to take.

I can never understand people who need to take drugs and any prison in the country is rife with the stuff. But as you can imagine it is a lot easier to smuggle anything into an open prison than into a more secure institution. So consequently, as one is in dormitory-type cubicles in an open prison, one is constantly seeing people abuse themselves with drugs. You would have to put up with stupid, inane laughter for hours during the night from some halfwit who had got a bit of false courage through taking some substance or other.

That, and the constant spitting that seems to be part of being one of the boys, disgusted me. I remember a very charming lady who was on the Board of Visitors saying to me one day, 'Eric, why don't you take your meals in the dining-room?' I replied that on the few occasions I had walked into the dining-room I had seen a continual stream of saliva the whole way. I would then have to sit opposite some character who had never heard of the word manners, let alone possessed any. I found it easier to live on what I could get from the shop.

I went to the gym every day to work out, so with the exercise and meagre diet I went from sixteen and a half stone down to thirteen in about eight months. By the time I came out I was very fit indeed.

At last I came to that most dreadful of times – waiting for a possible parole. I knew that if I got it, I would be very lucky as I would have done only ten months of my sentence. When the day came I was sent for and told that I was being let out on my first available parole date. I was overjoyed. I phoned my wife to tell her the good news and then I was able to thank all of the people who had helped me get through that time without too many problems.

I had just three weeks left to do and I thought, at last I know where my happiness is going to lie. I knew I was never going to do anything again to risk losing my liberty. When the morning came and I walked out of that place and saw my wife standing by the car I was probably the happiest bloke on earth. Back at home I was greeted by my little son, who was playing with a neighbour's kids. On seeing me again he said, 'My dad's back from work!'

The one thing I knew I was leaving behind was an entirely different type of criminal from the men I had found it worth suffering with, years before. I just could not believe the conversations I had had to listen to night after night in the dormitory of Kirkham Prison. I was disgusted by the complete disregard shown by the majority of inmates for the misery that they had caused their victims, and the pleasure they got from relating stories showing the despicable habits of common house-breakers like themselves. Stories of excreting in people's beds – that always got a laugh from the other morons who enjoyed that type of behaviour – and the amount of vandalism that they had inflicted on their victims. The amazing thing to me was that such people would strut around the prison as though they were the bees' knees. I would remember my first years in prison when the common housebreaker, muggers of old people and ponces, those that lived off the immoral earnings of prostitution, were only considered to be just one step above the child molesters; they knew it and were very loath to talk about their crimes. When I watch elderly crime victims being interviewed on TV nowadays and realize that there are so many people totally confined to their homes, living in constant fear of some kind of assault on their person or property, and then I hear politicians saying that the only thing they can do is to try to contain it at its present level, I become angry. I can't help thinking there is only one end to it all and that is anarchy. God help the future generation.

CHAPTER TWENTY-THREE

Family Man – and the Yorkshire Dales

Whilst in Kirkham I'd done some serious thinking and made up my mind to write a book. I knew that I would have difficulty writing in prison, for various reasons, but I started to make notes of the different periods of my life. It was then that I began to realize what a strange life I had led. The principles that I had adopted were not really principles at all. The principles that I had been taught as a kid, by my parents and at school, the normal rules of living, were the real principles.

I found it all so strange when I started to think back. I remembered that, as a kid, I was proud I could stand on my own two feet and tackle a bully and would never dream of hitting a man when he was down. As I got older and used to the people who could only win if they were mob-handed, I thought, well at least I've got something about me that they don't have. It's funny how certain people can take pleasure out of saying '*We* beat him' and think that they had done something really good. That's the one good thing that has come out of all my violent past. I can only ever remember one guy beating me on my own, and when I think of that day, he's one of the few people who I've really respected. I've seen and known guys who I've respected over the years because of the way they conducted themselves, although most people wouldn't have given them a second thought. I've seen and known men who have established reputations as tough guys, but when it came to proving themselves they had no substance. I found I was now thinking more about the people who had been or were 'real' people although some of their stories may not be as exciting or as glamorous as those of the more notorious characters I have met.

It wasn't very long after my release from Kirkham that I decided to make a complete break and moved to Harrogate. In doing so I have been able to find complete peace with myself. At the age of sixty-one I became a father again to the most beautiful little girl. I love Yorkshire and the scenery is breathtaking for someone who has been brought up in London and spent a fair lump of time behind prison walls. We often drive out into the Dales and enjoy the sheer beauty of the landscape. It seems a far cry from Dartmoor's damp and dank surroundings and the stench that pervades every prison in this country.

I still like a drink now and then and I've been lucky enough to have found one of the nicest pubs in Harrogate, the Coach and Horses. It's friendly and the clientele, although quite diverse in their business and social activities, all seem to be one big happy family. Local artist Jerome Hirst is a regular, along with his dog Ben who is the only 'tapper' that comes into the pub. John, the governor, has been a good friend to me and his father Bob, who is now semi-retired from work but not from drinking, is typical of the old-type publican. A friendly greeting with a merry quip and smile is always waiting you there.

I have made several excellent friends from nearly the first day of arriving in Harrogate: Ken Bradley and his wife Pat, Jack Rycroft, Stuart Simpson without whom this book wouldn't have been finished by now, my pal John Coglan. It gives me a great feeling to know that I have settled with real friends. Some will be shocked when they read this, but they're an understanding lot in Yorkshire. I love them!

It would be easy for me to settle into my comparatively idyllic way of life and say that my past is all behind me. I have got it made, I'm happy, I have a lovely family and friends and I live in rather gentle surroundings. But the past has a habit of intruding, sometimes pleasantly. I recently went over to the East End to visit a friend of mine and was surprised to meet so many old faces, all of whom seemed to have settled down into some type of business activity. I met Connie Whitehead who had been sentenced, with the Kray twins, for helping to dispose of the body of Jack the Hat McVitie. I naturally asked him about it, and he assured me that most of the stuff that had been written about the whole affair was conjecture. This made more sense to me than some of the rubbish I'd read. Connie and Pat, his wife, came up north to stay with us along with Billy Cox and his family. We had a superb couple of days together at the Majestic Hotel in Harrogate. We would sit in the bar in the evening and talk about the old days. It was a far cry from those times when we were all dashing around looking for something that wasn't there.

Meeting Connie also made me realize how lucky I am, particularly when I think how many years my life has spanned and realize that the Kray twins have been locked up for nearly half that time. Many people I meet pose the question, 'Why do they keep them still locked up after all of these years?' It always starts a debate and the usual comparisons arise. 'They let out child killers after a comparatively short time.' This is not strictly true as the notorious child killers always do long stretches in jail. But many people sentenced to life imprisonment are released in a lot less time than the Kray twins have done and are still doing. To the ordinary man in the street it is difficult to see the reasoning behind this.

I have my own opinions about why the Krays have spent so long in prison, and it is a simple question of the judiciary wanting to have the last word. When the Krays were tried nobody was interested in the actual killings or the people who were killed. The men standing in the dock and the victims were all villains who had come from the back streets of the city. They had had squabbles that resulted in the deaths of a couple of people no one would miss. But then came the trial, at that time the longest murder trial in British penal history, and it caught the imagination of the public so that every word in the case was followed diligently and the myth of the Krays was born nationwide. When Ronnie Kray's famous outburst to the prosecution counsel accusing him of being a 'fat slob' was reported in every newspaper in the country, it ensured that the architect of the remark would do the longest sentence for contempt of court that has ever been delivered.

I have spent many years inside and believe that I understand the amount of damage prison can do to an individual. One can only admire the way the Krays have done a quarter of a century in various prisons with dignity. I have recently received a number of letters from Reggie

Kray and it amazes me that he still has his sense of humour. I sent him some photos of my family, taken whilst on picnic trips and in the garden. His next letter was so poignant. He thought I was lucky to have come through all of my problems and to have such a lovely family. He went on to talk of people who he thinks are less fortunate than himself, such as the kids that have been born with no chance of having a full life because of certain illnesses. I offered to write to people who would have some say in his release, telling them about the help he gives these kids but he said, 'No, under no circumstances do I want to be released because of a few gestures that I have made.' But I know that what he desires most is to be able to finish his life in the type of surroundings that I have been lucky enough to find myself.

It would be interesting to see under the new proposed rules regarding the parole system, how the Parole Board would look at the case of Reggie Kray. I could not visualize how any person who was in a responsible position and who looked at his case dispassionately would fail to recognize that enough was enough. I remember well the reputation that the twins had in the late fifties and early sixties. Every local villain knew that you didn't mess about with the twins but at the same time every local trader and man on the street knew he was safe from being molested or mugged. A very different world from today. People who had hard times knew that they could always go to see the twins and receive a helping hand.

I often think back to the days when I knew the Kray twins well and I think I am intelligent enough to know the difference between good and evil. I have met many evil people but although the Kray brothers were tough, typical products of wartime East End London, they had in a way more principles than many people with more privileged upbringing. The type of gangland incident that they were involved in was just a natural progression of the only way of life that they had grown up in. So in that sense they were not evil, unlike a person that preys on the misery of others. I can assure you the Kray twins would be welcomed into the houses of some of the victims of horrible crimes more readily than some criminals who have not received half the punishment that the Krays have.

I think Reggie has got a lot to offer. I'm sure if people could hear Reggie talking today they would realize that he has not wasted his time, and Ronnie has proved that with medication he could lead a normal life, he would never be a threat to the public at large, he never has been.

I knew the victims that the Krays were sent to prison for killing and one of them was once my best friend. I am sure that if Jack McVitie – 'Jack the Hat' – could speak now he would say, 'They've done their bird, like men, let them go now.'